ELINES
OF
HISTORY

VOLUME 7

ROYALTY AND REVOLT

1600–1700

GROLIER

an imprint of

■SCHOLASTIC

www.scholastic.com/librarypublishing

Published by Grolier,
an imprint of Scholastic Library Publishing,
Sherman Turnpike
Danbury, Connecticut 06816

© 2005 The Brown Reference Group plc

Set ISBN 0-7172-6002-X
Volume 7 ISBN 0-7172-6009-7

Library of Congress Cataloging-in-Publication Data

Timelines of history.
    p. cm.
    Includes index.
    Contents: v. 1. The early empires, prehistory—500 B.C. —
v. 2. The classical age, 500 B.C.—500 A.D. — v. 3. Raiders and
conquerors, 500—1000 — v. 4. The feudal era, 1000—1250 —
v. 5. The end of the Middle Ages, 1250—1500 — v. 6. A wider
world, 1500—1600 — v. 7. Royalty and revolt, 1600—1700 —
v. 8. The Age of Reason, 1700—1800 — v. 9. Industry and
empire, 1800—1900 — v. 10. The modern world, 1900—2000.
    ISBN 0-7172-6002-X (set : alk. paper) — ISBN 0-7172-
6003-8 (v. 1 : alk. paper) — ISBN 0-7172-6004-6 (v. 2 : alk.
paper) — ISBN 0-7172-6005-4 (v. 3 : alk. paper) — ISBN 0-
7172-6006-2 (v. 4 : alk. paper) — ISBN 0-7172-6007-0 (v. 5 :
alk. paper) — ISBN 0-7172-6008-9 (v. 6 : alk. paper) — ISBN
0-7172-6009-7 (v. 7 : alk. paper) — ISBN 0-7172-6010-0 (v. 8
: alk.paper) — ISBN 0-7172-6011-9 (v. 9 : alk. paper) —
ISBN 0-7172-6012-7 (v. 10 : alk. paper)
    1. Chronology, Historical

For information address the publisher:
Grolier, Sherman Turnpike,
Danbury, Connecticut 06816

Printed and bound in Thailand

FOR THE BROWN REFERENCE GROUP PLC

Consultant: Professor Jeremy Black, Exeter University

Project Editor: Tony Allan
Designers: Frankie Wood
Picture Researcher: Sharon Southren
Cartographic Editor: Tim Williams
Design Manager: Lynne Ross
Production: Alastair Gourlay, Maggie Copeland
Editorial Director: Lindsey Lowe
Senior Managing Editor: Tim Cooke
Writers: Susan Kennedy, Michael Kerrigan, Peter Lewis

CONTENTS

HOW TO USE THIS BOOK

INTRODUCTION

Royalty and Revolt covers a time when the institution of monarchy was at its height across much of the globe. In Europe the 17th century was the epoch of France's Louis XIV, the Sun King, whose radiance illuminated one of the most magnificent courts the continent had ever seen. In Asia Persia's Shah Abbas restored something of the glory of the Sassanid kings who had ruled the nation 1,000 years before. The Manchu Emperor Kangxi occupied the throne for 60 years, bringing China an age of peace and stability rarely matched in its long dynastic history.

Yet beneath the surface fresh currents were stirring. European explorers and settlers were on the move, opening up new territory in North America and Oceania, while Cossack adventurers traveling by boat, horse, and sledge blazed a trail into the Russian Far East. Intellectual horizons were widening too as the Scientific Revolution gathered pace, opening up radically new vistas of the nature of the universe by the time the century drew to a close.

Some of this ferment found its way into the political arena, challenging the very basis of royal authority that elsewhere seemed so secure. Kangxi only came to the throne after the preceding Ming Dynasty rulers had been violently ejected from power. In Britain a king lost his head to Parliamentarian rebels, while in the Netherlands too people decided that they could do without a monarch when they founded the Dutch Republic. Only Japan swam against the tide of change, cutting itself off from the West by imperial decree and choosing instead to isolate itself within its own traditions.

ABBREVIATIONS
mi	miles
cm	centimeters
m	meters
km	kilometers
sq. km	square kilometers
mya	million years ago
c.	about (from the Latin word circa)

A NOTE ON DATES
This set follows standard Western practice in dating events from the start of the Christian era, presumed to have begun in the year 0. Those that happened before the year 0 are listed as B.C. (before the Christian era), and those that happened after as A.D. (from the Latin Anno Domini, meaning "in the year of the Lord"). Wherever possible, exact dates are given; where there is uncertainty, the date is prefixed by the abbreviation c. (short for Latin circa, meaning "about") to show that it is approximate.

ABOUT THIS SET

This book is one of a set of ten providing timelines for world history from the beginning of recorded history up to 2000 A.D. Each volume arranges events that happened around the world within a particular period and is made up of three different types of facing two-page spreads: timelines, features, and glossary pages ("Facts at a Glance," at the back of the book). The three should be used in combination to find the information that you need. Timelines list events that occurred between the dates shown on the pages and cover periods ranging from several centuries at the start of Volume 1, dealing with early times, to six or seven years in Volumes 9 and 10, addressing the modern era.

In part, the difference reflects the fact that much more is known about recent times than about distant eras. Yet it also reflects a real acceleration in the number of noteworthy events, related to surging population growth. Demographers estimate that it was only in the early 19th century that world population reached one billion; at the start of the 21st century the figure is over six billion and rising, meaning that more people have lived in the past 200 years than in all the other epochs of history combined.

The subjects covered by the feature pages may be a major individual or a civilization. Some cover epoch-making events, while others address more general themes such as the development of types of technology. In each case the feature provides a clear overview of its subject to supplement its timeline entries, indicating its significance on the broader canvas of world history.

Facts at a Glance lists names and terms that may be unfamiliar or that deserve more explanation than can be provided in the timeline entries. Check these pages for quick reference on individuals, peoples, battles, or cultures, and also for explanations of words that are not clear.

The comprehensive index at the back of each book covers the entire set and will enable you to follow all references to a given subject across the ten volumes.

TIMELINE PAGES

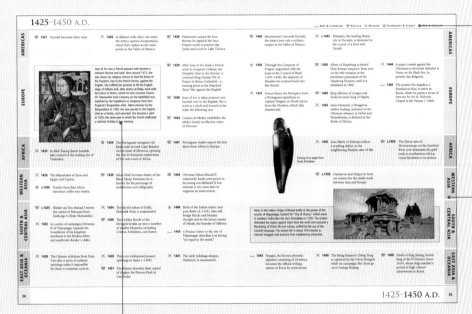

Symbols
Each entry is prefixed by one of five symbols—for example, crossed swords for war, an open book for arts and literature—indicating a particular category of history. A key to the symbols is printed at the top of the right-hand page.

Bands
Each timeline is divided into five or six bands relating to different continents or other major regions of the world. Within each band events are listed in chronological (time) order.

Boxes
Boxes in each timeline present more detailed information about important individuals, places, events, or works.

FEATURE PAGES

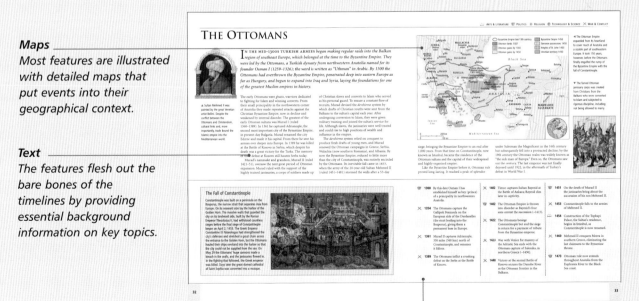

Maps
Most features are illustrated with detailed maps that put events into their geographical context.

Text
The features flesh out the bare bones of the timelines by providing essential background information on key topics.

Subject-specific timelines
Each feature has a timeline devoted exclusively to its topic to give an at-a-glance overview of the main developments in its history.

1600–1610 A.D.

AMERICAS

⊛ **1602** Sebastian Vizcaino sails from Acapulco, Mexico, along the coast of California but fails to discover San Francisco Bay.

⊛ **1606** The Plymouth Company is founded in London with the object of establishing colonies in North America; two unsuccessful expeditions are sent this year.

♛ **1607** Captain John Smith founds the Jamestown colony at the mouth of the James River in Virginia.

♛ **1608** French explorer Samuel de Champlain founds a colony at Quebec.

EUROPE

✴ **1600** Italian scientist and one-time friar Giordano Bruno is burned at the stake in Rome for his heretical views concerning the nature of the universe.

♛ **1603** On the death of Queen Elizabeth I, James VI of Scotland becomes King James I of England, uniting the two kingdoms.

In a time of religious tension in England the Gunpowder Plot was the most lethal threat to the nation's ruling class. In 1605 a small group of Catholics (right) conspired to blow up the Houses of Parliament while the Protestant King James I of England was there. Assigned to ignite the gunpowder, Guido, or Guy, Fawkes was arrested just before he did so. His effigy is still burned on Bonfire Night each November 5.

AFRICA

Wooden figurine by the Luba people of central Africa.

♛ **c. 1600** The empire of Mwene Mutapa—the successor state of Great Zimbabwe in southeastern Africa—is at its greatest extent.

♛ **c.1605** The Kingdom of Luba is by now beginning to emerge as an economic and political power in central Africa.

WESTERN ASIA

⚔ **1602** Shah Abbas of Persia begins a campaign to win back the Safavid lands in Iraq from the Ottoman Empire.

♛ **1603** Ahmed I becomes Ottoman sultan.

♛ **1606** The Ottomans sign the treaty of Zsitvatörök with Austria, in which they are forced to recognize the Hapsburg emperor as an equal and grant trading concessions to Europeans.

SOUTH & CENTRAL ASIA

♛ **1601** Salim, son of the Mughal Emperor Akbar, rebels against his father but is later restored to favor (–1604).

♛ **1605** Akbar dies and is succeeded as emperor by Salim, who takes the title of Jahangir.

⚔ **1605** Jahangir orders the execution of the fifth Sikh guru, Arjun, for his part in supporting a rebellion led by Prince Khusrau, Jahangir's son.

EAST ASIA & OCEANIA

♛ **1600** In Myanmar (Burma) the state of Pegu collapses, and the country fragments into a number of small states.

♛ **1600** After winning the Battle of Sekigahara, Ieyasu of the Tokugawa clan becomes the virtual ruler of Japan.

⊛ **1602** An English trading station is established at Bantam in Java (Indonesia).

⊕ **1609** Henry Hudson enters New York Bay and sails up the river that will later be named for him as far as the future site of Albany.

Shown in this fanciful illustration leading an attack on a fortified Iroquois village, Samuel de Champlain did more than anyone else to establish a French presence in North America. He led pioneering expeditions up the St. Lawrence River, founded Quebec, and ended his life as governor of New France, the colony set up in the lands he had explored.

✕ **1604** The "Time of Troubles," a period of civil war in Russia, begins when a pretender, Dmitry, claims to be czar and wins widespread support from the Cossacks.

🏛 **1604** In Hungary an alliance between Protestants and an Ottoman army led by Istvan Bocskay forces the Hapsburgs to withdraw from Transylvania.

📖 **1605** In Spain Miguel de Cervantes publishes the first book of his masterpiece *Don Quixote*.

🏛 **1605** In England conspirators attempt to blow up the Houses of Parliament, but their Gunpowder Plot is discovered.

✕ **1609** The United Provinces of the Netherlands agree on a 12-year truce with Spain.

🏛 **1609** Sweden gains Karelia (part of modern Finland) in return for supporting Boris, the new czar, in the civil war in Russia.

⊕ **1609** German astronomer Johannes Kepler publishes his first two laws of planetary motion, which show that the planets travel in elliptical paths around the sun.

☀ **1609** King Philip III orders the expulsion of the Moriscos (Christianized descendants of the Arabs) from Spain, an act of ethnic cleansing that sees more than 300,000 people forcibly deported in the next five years.

🏛 **c.1605** A dynasty of rulers, probably immigrants from East Africa, establishes a Merina state in the central highlands of Madagascar.

🏛 **1605** Rebels kill the Ottoman governor of Egypt.

📖 **1609** Construction begins on the Mosque of Ahmed I (more often known as the Blue Mosque) in Istanbul.

The Blue Mosque was the last of Istanbul's great imperial mosques to be built.

🏛 **1606** Jahangir has Khusrau blinded and many of his followers killed.

⊕ **1608** English envoys land at Surat on India's east coast, seeking to negotiate trading rights.

🏛 **1603** Ieyasu is formally appointed shogun (military ruler); his stronghold Edo (modern Tokyo) becomes the center of power in Japan.

✕ **1605** The Dutch seize the Indonesian island of Amboina from the Portuguese; it will become the center of the spice trade to Europe.

1600–1610 A.D.

AMERICAS

EUROPE

AFRICA

WESTERN ASIA

SOUTH & CENTRAL ASIA

EAST ASIA & OCEANIA

PERSIA'S GREAT SHAH

▲ Persia's Safavid Dynasty owed its hold on power to Turkmen warriors like this one.

▼ A fresco from a palace ceiling shows Shah Abbas receiving foreign envoys.

ABBAS I WAS THE MOST EFFECTIVE RULER OF PERSIA *since ancient times. He restored the fortunes of the Safavid Dynasty when they had fallen to a low ebb and secured the country's frontiers against the Ottomans and Uzbeks. He revived trade and encouraged merchants, craftsmen, and artists to settle in his new capital of Esfahan, which he transformed into one of the largest and most beautiful cities in the world.*

The Safavids were Sufis, members of an Islamic mystic order based at Ardabil, west of the Caspian Sea. The traditional leaders of the Turkmen tribes in this northwest corner of Persia, they embraced military conquest as a means of spreading the Shia branch of Islam to which they and their followers belonged. By 1502 Esmail I, the head of the order, was strong enough to declare himself shah (ruler) of Persia and to embark on a campaign of conquest. A great variety of peoples inhabited Persia at the time—Kurds, Armenians, and Arabs, as well as Turkmens and Persians—and Esmail I made Shiism the state religion as a means of imposing his authority on them.

The Ottoman rulers to the west of Persia and the Uzbeks to the northeast belonged to the Sunni branch of Islam, and Esmail's successors faced continual harassment from both of them. By the time that Abbas I came to the throne in 1588, the Safavids had lost considerable territory, and their authority was further weakened by intertribal factions and jealousy.

Abbas realized that he could not fight on two fronts at once. In 1590 he signed an unfavorable peace treaty with the Ottomans in order to leave himself free to deal with the Uzbeks. At the same time, he set about creating a strong, permanent army recruited mainly from non-Muslim Georgians, Armenians, and Circassians. Called *ghulums* ("slaves"), they converted to Islam and were then trained for the army or the royal administration like the janissaries, their equivalents in the Ottoman Empire. Abbas preferred the *ghulums* for high office over local tribal leaders whose loyalty was unreliable.

Esfahan, Abbas's capital

In 1597, soon after his defeat of the Uzbeks, Abbas decided to move his capital from Qazvin, which was dangerously close to the Ottoman war zone, to the small town of Esfahan in central Persia. Esfahan had briefly served as the nation's capital in the 11th and 12th centuries but had subsequently fallen into decline. Now the shah determined to rebuild it on a scale fitting his political ambitions. Over the next two decades he endowed it with stately, tree-lined avenues, ornamental fountains, palaces, bazaars, public buildings, and gardens. Visitors to the city marveled at its 162 mosques, 48 colleges, and 273 public baths. At its center was an immense open space, the Maidan, that was seven times larger than St. Mark's Square in Venice. The Royal Mosque, decorated with blue enameled tiles, stood on one side of this arena, while the Mosque of Sheikh Lutfallah, reserved for the shah's private devotions, occupied another. On a third stood the entrance to the central bazaar, painted with murals showing Abbas's victories over the Uzbeks. At the square's end a great gate led to a series of gardens and to a long boulevard, the Chahar Bagh, lined with parks, palaces, and pavilions for the royal family and nobles of the court.

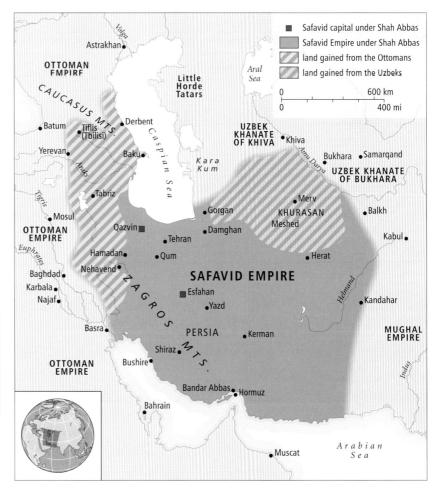

Abbas engaged an English adventurer, Sir Anthony Sherley, to train his new army in artillery tactics. Once he had expelled the Uzbeks from Khurasan he turned his attention to the Ottomans, winning back Baghdad, Mosul, and most of Iraq in a series of campaigns. Sir Robert Sherley, Anthony's brother, also became a close adviser, and in 1609 Abbas sent him on a mission to a number of European countries to try and win their support for a military alliance against the Ottomans.

During Abbas's reign Persia grew rich through its monopoly of the silk trade. A discerning patron of the arts, Abbas invited craftsmen and artists to settle in Persia, and he encouraged the production of textiles, carpets, and ceramics. Like his contemporaries the Mughal Emperor Akbar and Queen Elizabeth I of England, he presided over a great court at his capital of Esfahan, where he welcomed ambassadors and merchants from many European countries. He was open to new ideas and enjoyed discussing religious theories with foreign visitors. Unusually for an Islamic ruler, he allowed Christians to wear what they liked and to own property in Esfahan.

▲ Shah Abbas's foreign policy was dominated by wars against the Ottomans to the west and the Uzbeks to the east. He won large swaths of territory from each, building a Persian empire larger than any known since antiquity.

♨ **1588** Abbas I, third son of Mohammed Shah, succeeds him on his death.	♨ **1602** Abbas breaks his treaty with the Ottomans.	✕ **1622** Abbas ousts the Portuguese from the island of Hormuz at the entrance to the Persian Gulf.
♨ **1590** Abbas makes peace on unfavorable terms with the Ottoman Empire.	📖 **1603** The Mosque of Sheikh Lutfallah is built in Esfahan (–1619).	✕ **1623** In a major offensive against the Ottomans Abbas wins back Baghdad and establishes control over the Shia holy cities of Najaf and Karbala in Iraq (–1624).
✕ **1598** Abbas defeats the Uzbeks and recovers Khurasan and Herat; he moves his capital to Esfahan.	♨ **1609** Abbas sends Sir Robert Sherley on an embassy to Europe.	
✕ **1599** Sir Anthony Sherley arrives in Persia; he will be put in charge of training Abbas's army.	📖 **1611** Work begins on the Royal Mosque.	♨ **1629** Death of Abbas.

A later painting shows indigenous people greeting the explorer Henry Hudson in the course of one of his North American voyages.

AMERICAS

1610 English explorer Henry Hudson discovers the bay in Canada that now bears his name; he disappears the following year after being set adrift by mutineers.

1610 The first Dutch settlers from New Jersey arrive on Manhattan Island, founding the colony of New Amsterdam (New York).

EUROPE

1610 In the Plantation of Ulster, King James I of England encourages thousands of Scottish Protestants to settle in Catholic northern Ireland, creating a lasting religious divide.

1610 Henry IV of France is assassinated in Paris by a religious fanatic. He is succeeded by the nine-year-old Louis XIII, whose mother Marie de Medicis rules as regent under the guidance of Cardinal Richelieu.

1611 The King James Bible—the first authorized English translation—is published in London.

1611 Gustavus II Adolphus ascends the Swedish throne, starting Sweden's rise to become a major European power.

1613 Russia's Time of Troubles ends when Michael I is elected czar; a Romanov, his dynasty will last until the Russian Empire collapses in 1917.

1614 The Estates-General, France's administrative assembly since 1347, meets for the last time until 1789, marking the start of absolute monarchy in France.

1615 Spanish writer Miguel de Cervantes completes his epic novel *Don Quixote*.

1616 William Shakespeare, England's greatest playwright, dies in Stratford-upon-Avon aged 52.

AFRICA

1610 Ralambo takes power as the last ruler of the Merina people of highland Madagascar before French settlement begins.

1610 Queen Amina of the Hausa people dies after extending her West African empire south to the Niger Delta.

1612 Moroccan forces withdraw from western Sudan but retain control over the declining Songhai Empire east of the Sahara.

WESTERN ASIA

1614 Cossack pirates sack and burn Sinope on Turkey's northern coast; the Ottomans lose control of the Black Sea.

1616 Renewed warfare breaks out between the Ottomans and the armies of Persia's Shah Abbas.

SOUTH & CENTRAL ASIA

c.1610 With the defeat of the southern Toungou realm the Kingdom of Ava becomes the dominant force in Myanmar (Burma).

This gold commemorative coin issued by the Mughal Emperor Jahangir bears a portrait of his father Akbar.

EAST ASIA & OCEANIA

1612 Japanese Shogun Tokugawa Ieyasu outlaws Christianity, launching a persecution of converts and ordering all Christian missionaries to leave the country.

1614 Ieyasu lays siege to and captures Osaka Castle, ending a challenge to his rule from the warlord Hideyori (–1615).

1615 Nurhachi, leader of the Juchen (Manchu) people, unites the tribes on China's northeast frontier, laying the groundwork for his later conquest of China and the founding of the Manchu (Qing) Dynasty.

👑 **1611** Native American princess Pocahontas marries Jamestown settler John Rolfe, bringing a truce in the war between English settlers and the Algonquians.

⊕ **1615** Rubber and drinking chocolate are first exported from the Americas to Europe.

⊕ **1616** Willem Schouten, a Dutch East India Company captain, rounds the southern tip of South America, naming it Kap Hoorn (Cape Horn) after his hometown in the Netherlands.

👑 **1619** The first shipment of African "indentured laborers" to Jamestown, Virginia, heralds the start of the slave trade in North America.

👑 **1619** The first Thanksgiving Day is celebrated by settlers at Hampton, Virginia.

AMERICAS

⊕ **1616** Denounced as a heretic for confirming Copernicus's observation that the Earth moves round the sun, Galileo Galilei is barred from scientific study by the Catholic church.

✕ **1618** The Thirty Years' War begins with an uprising in Bohemia against Hapsburg rule after Protestant governors are thrown from a window at Hradcany Castle in the "Defenestration of Prague."

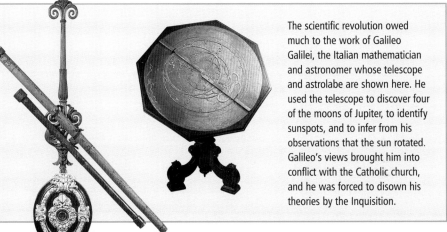

The scientific revolution owed much to the work of Galileo Galilei, the Italian mathematician and astronomer whose telescope and astrolabe are shown here. He used the telescope to discover four of the moons of Jupiter, to identify sunspots, and to infer from his observations that the sun rotated. Galileo's views brought him into conflict with the Catholic church, and he was forced to disown his theories by the Inquisition.

EUROPE

✕ **1614** A Portuguese fleet bombards the palace of the Sultan of Mombasa in what is now Kenya; the sultan visits Goa to protest.

⊕ **1619** More than 300,000 Egyptians fall victim to a plague epidemic.

AFRICA

👑 **1617** Ottoman Sultan Ahmed I dies and is succeeded by his brother Mustafa I, aged 26.

👑 **1618** Mustafa is declared unfit to govern and is replaced as Ottoman ruler by Osman II.

👑 **1618** Peace is restored with Persia when the Ottomans agree to abandon Azerbaijan and Georgia.

WESTERN ASIA

👑 **1611** The Mughal Emperor Jahangir marries Nur Jahan, who becomes a leading figure in the royal household and effectively rules India until the death of her husband.

✕ **1612** Forces of the English East India Company defeat a Portuguese fleet off Surat in Gujarat, western India, going on to establish the first permanent trading post ("factory") in India at the port.

👑 **1618** Birth of Aurangzeb, future ruler of India, under whose control the Mughal Empire will reach its greatest extent.

SOUTH & CENTRAL ASIA

⊕ **1616** Porcelain manufacture begins in Japan when imported Korean potters discover a kaolin deposit on the island of Kyushu.

👑 **1616** English involvement in the Southeast Asian spice trade gets under way when Nathaniel Courthope forms an alliance with the people of Banda Island in the Moluccas and withstands a four-year siege by Dutch forces.

👑 **1619** Batavia (modern Jakarta) on Java becomes the administrative center of the Dutch East India Company for its trade and plantation operations in Southeast Asia.

EAST ASIA & OCEANIA

1610–1620 A.D.

SETTLING NORTH AMERICA

B EFORE THE 17TH CENTURY THE EUROPEAN POWERS *made few systematic attempts to settle North America. Early explorers went searching for riches or a northwest passage to East Asia. Spanish conquistadors looked in vain in the south for the fabled realm of gold, El Dorado, while far to the north the French sailor Jacques Cartier explored the St. Lawrence River from 1534 to 1541. By the late 1630s, however, several different European groups had gained a firm foothold along the eastern seaboard.*

▲ Relations between the European settlers and the indigenous peoples they met in the New World were usually hostile. This figure of a bow-wielding warrior decorated a Massachussets weather vane.

The fate of the first English colony in North America is shrouded in mystery. A small settlement was established at Roanoke Island off the Virginia coast in 1584 and was reinforced by the famed adventurer Walter Raleigh, who sent more settlers in 1587. Yet when a relief party arrived three years later, no trace survived of the colony's 120 inhabitants.

No one knows whether Roanoke was wiped out by violence, illness, or famine, but all of these were real threats to other early colonists. English settlers at Jamestown, founded in Virginia in 1607, faced malaria, hostile indigenous people, and hunger, and almost abandoned the site. The planting of tobacco eventually assured the colony's prosperity; by 1619 some 50,000 pounds (22,500 kg) of the "sot-weed" hated by King James I were being exported to England. A more sinister trade began the same year when the first African slaves were landed from a Dutch ship. But life in Jamestown remained fragile; in 1622 a massive attack by a native alliance known as the Powhatan Confederacy left 350 men, women, and children dead. In turn, imported diseases such as smallpox, typhoid, and malaria took a terrible toll on the native population.

At around the same time, French settlers under Samuel de Champlain came into conflict with the local Iroquois in the Great Lakes area. Yet Champlain forged amicable fur trading links with the Iroquois' traditional enemies, the Huron and Algonquian peoples. This alliance was to serve the French well in their war against the English in the following century.

European settlement began to focus on the Northeast from the 1620s on. In 1626 Peter Minuit, acting for the Dutch West India Company, bought Manhattan Island from the native Wappinger people and founded the town of New Amsterdam (later New York). The wider colony of New Netherland arose in the area between the Hudson and Connecticut rivers but never thrived, as Holland neglected it in favor of its East Asian interests.

✹ **1540** Conquistador Francisco Coronado leads an expedition north from Mexico into southwestern North America (–1541).

👑 **1566** St. Augustine, the first European settlement on mainland North America, is founded as a military outpost in Florida by Spanish explorer Menéndez de Avilés.

👑 **1584** Walter Raleigh founds a colony on Roanoke Island, Virginia; the colony fails, and all trace of it has disappeared by the time a relief expedition arrives in 1590.

👑 **1607** The first continuous English settlement is founded by the London Company at Jamestown in Virginia; the colony supports itself through tobacco growing.

✹ **1608** Exploring the St. Lawrence River, French explorer Samuel de Champlain establishes the colony of New France at Quebec, later becoming its commandant.

👑 **1619** The first elections are held in the colonies when 22 "burgesses" are elected to the Virginia Assembly by popular vote in Jamestown.

☀ **1620** The Pilgrims arrive at Cape Cod, Massachusetts, aboard the *Mayflower*; they choose New Plymouth as the site of the first Puritan colony.

✕ **1622** The Powhatan Confederacy, a group of Algonquian-speaking peoples, attacks European settlements in Virginia, killing over 350 settlers.

✹ **1624** Dutch merchants establish the colony of Fort Orange (Albany) up the Hudson River, predominantly to trade furs with the Iroquois Confederacy.

✹ **1626** Fort Amsterdam (later New Amsterdam) is founded on the tip of Manhattan Island by Dutch traders.

👑 **1630** A large colonizing expedition sets sail from England, founding Boston, Massachusetts, and six other towns nearby.

✕ **1637** Mystic, Connecticut, is destroyed by a mixed Narragansett, Pequot, and Mohican force, and over 600 inhabitants are massacred.

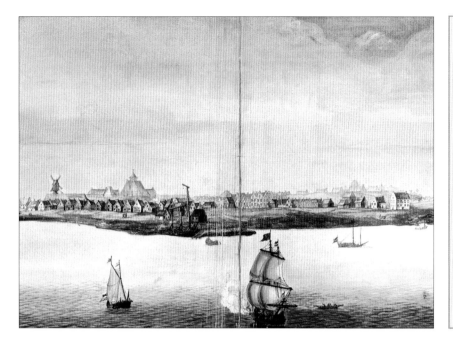

Pocahontas

As the Jamestown colonists began to starve, their leader, Captain John Smith, went upcountry from Chesapeake Bay in 1607 to barter for corn with the Algonquian people. Received with hostility and facing death, Smith was saved when Chief Powhatan's 12-year-old daughter Pocahontas pleaded for his life. Five years later she was herself taken as a captive to Jamestown, where she met the settler John Rolfe, marrying him in 1614. Rolfe took his wife, who had converted to Christianity and changed her name to Rebecca, back to England in 1616. There she was presented to the king and society, and was received with great curiosity and acclaim, but died of smallpox as she embarked on the return journey. Pocahontas is often seen as symbolizing harmony between different peoples; violence and exploitation, however, marked most settlers' response to Native Americans.

Commercial concerns were the driving force behind the earliest settlements, but a very different kind of settler soon arrived in growing numbers. Fleeing persecution in England, a group of Puritan religious dissenters set sail for the New World to create a community where they could practice their faith in peace. These Pilgrims founded the Plymouth Colony on Cape Cod in 1620. The Mayflower Compact, named for their ship, agreed to establish a "civil body politic" based on the will of the majority—an early expression of American democracy.

▲ A painting by the Dutch artist Johannes Vinckeboons shows how Manhattan Island looked in the early days when it was occupied by Dutch settlers and known as New Amsterdam rather than New York.

▼ The European settlement of North America began on the East Coast. Settlers from England, France, Sweden, and the Netherlands carved out terrritories, contesting the land with each other and with indigenous peoples.

1643 The New England Confederation, the first union of English colonies in America, is founded for mutual defense against Dutch and French settlers and hostile indigenous peoples.

1664 English troops seize New Amsterdam from the Dutch and rename it New York.

1671 English settlers are the first Europeans to cross the Appalachian Mountains.

1675 Chief Metacomet, known to colonists as King Philip, leads the Narragansett and Wampanoag peoples in an uprising against New England settlements, killing some 600 colonists (–1676).

1681 William Penn begins to establish Quaker colonies in North America.

AMERICAS

The Pilgrims who sailed from England on the *Mayflower* and settled at Cape Cod were the first permanent European settlers of New England. Some had been persecuted for their Puritan views and had first sought refuge in the Netherlands. Granted permission by the British government to settle in America, they were able to make the trip with the aid of financial backing from London merchants.

1620 The *Mayflower* arrives in Cape Cod, Massachusetts, carrying 102 settlers, including Puritans fleeing religious persecution in England.

1621 Potatoes, native to the Andes Mountains region of South America, reach Europe for the first time and are planted in Germany.

EUROPE

1620 At the Battle of the White Mountain near Prague a Catholic army defeats a Bohemian force led by Frederick V in the first major engagement of the Thirty Years' War.

1620 Sweden's Gustavus II Adolphus overruns Livonia (modern Latvia and Lithuania) and drives out Polish forces (–1629).

1620 Dutch engineer Cornelius Drebbel tests the first submarine, built of wood and leather.

1624 Cardinal Richelieu is appointed first minister by Louis XIII, becoming the most powerful political figure in France.

AFRICA

c.1620 The Akan Kingdom of Denkyera emerges as a growing power in the forested lands north of the Gold Coast.

1624 Queen Nzinga comes to power in Matamba (Angola); she will check Portuguese expansion inland from coastal slaving bases.

1626 French explorer Thomas Lambart makes landfall at the mouth of the Senegal River in West Africa.

WESTERN ASIA

1622 Persian forces in alliance with troops provided by the English East India Company capture the important trading base at Hormuz at the mouth of the Persian Gulf, under Portuguese control since 1507.

1622 Osman II tries to suppress the growing power of the janissaries (the elite palace guard of the Ottoman Empire) but is murdered by them.

1623 Murad IV, Osman's nephew, becomes Ottoman sultan and moves to crush the janissaries.

SOUTH & CENTRAL ASIA

1625 The Mughals under Emperor Jahangir lose control of the strategically important city of Kandahar in what is now Afghanistan to the Persian Safavid Empire.

A cameo brooch in gold, enamel, and sardonyx shows the Mughal Emperor Shah Jahan killing a lion.

EAST ASIA & OCEANIA

1621 The expansion of the Manchu people of Manchuria begins when Nurhachi, their leader, seizes land in northeastern China, including the city of Shenyang; renamed Mukden, it will become his capital (–1625).

1622 Dutch traders found a fortified settlement on the offshore Chinese island of Formosa (today's Taiwan).

1623 Dutch–English rivalry in Southeast Asia intensifies as 12 English traders are killed when Dutch troops sack Amboina on the island of Ceram (Moluccas).

⊕ **1621** James I of England (author of *A Counterblast to Tobacco*) sends an emissary on a failed mission to persuade Virginia colonists not to grow tobacco.

✕ **1622** Native American warriors of the Powhatan Confederacy attack Virginia settlements, killing around 350 colonists.

✕ **1623** Dutch raiders seize the ports of Pernambuco (Recife) and Bahia, the capital of Brazil, from the Portuguese, who regain control shortly after (–1625).

⊕ **1626** Fur traders in the service of the Dutch West India Company found New Amsterdam on Manhattan Island.

✕ **1626** Dutch admiral Piet Hein intercepts a Spanish bullion flotilla off Cuba, seizing a fortune in Peruvian silver.

〰 **1625** James I of England dies and is succeeded by his son Charles I.

✕ **1625** Christian IV of Denmark intervenes on the Protestant side in the Thirty Years' War (–1629).

✕ **1628** Richelieu's troops capture the Huguenot (Protestant) stronghold of La Rochelle after a long siege.

⊕ **1628** English physician William Harvey publishes *On the Motion of the Heart and Blood*, a pioneering study of the circulatory system.

〰 **1629** Charles I of England dissolves Parliament and rules as an absolute monarch (–1640).

✕ **1629** Denmark is forced to withdraw from the Thirty Years' War following defeats by Catholic forces under von Wallenstein.

⊕ **1626** The first French colonists settle on the island of Madagascar.

⊕ **1629** Portuguese settlers in Angola plant corn and cassava from America; the crops will become staples of the African diet.

Shown here wearing ceremonial headgear, the janissaries were fearsome soldiers, the shock troops of the Ottoman Empire. Recruited largely from Balkan Christian families and forcibly converted to Islam, they owed their loyalty directly to the state. From the 17th century on they took an active part in politics, frequently making and unmaking sultans.

✕ **1623** Shah Abbas I of Persia completes his conquest of Iraq (begun in 1603) with the capture of Mosul and Baghdad from the Ottoman Empire (–1624).

〰 **1629** Shah Abbas dies and is succeeded by his grandson Safi I, aged 13.

☀ **1627** The first Westerners—two Jesuit missionaries—arrive in the Himalayan kingdom of Bhutan.

〰 **1627** Emperor Jahangir dies, to be succeeded by his son Shah Jahan.

〰 **1629** Uzbeks take over the city and region of Kandahar after the defection of the Persian governor.

〰 **1623** Shogun Hidetada of Japan abdicates in favor of his son Iemitsu; the persecution of Christians continues.

✕ **1627** Manchu troops invade Korea and force it to become a vassal state.

✕ **1627** Peasant rebellions protesting harsh taxation by Ming rulers break out in central and northern China, and rapidly become widespread (–1644).

✕ **1628** From their enclave at Batavia the Dutch launch repeated attacks to spread their power across Java, now ruled by Sultan Agung of Mataram.

AMERICAS

EUROPE

AFRICA

WESTERN ASIA

SOUTH & CENTRAL ASIA

EAST ASIA & OCEANIA

1620–1630 A.D.

THE THIRTY YEARS' WAR

▲ Sweden's King Gustavus II Adolphus turned the tide of the war in the Protestants' favor when he intervened in 1630. When he was killed in battle two years later, imperial armies regained the initiative.

▶ The Treaty of Westphalia, which finally brought the war to an end, took four years to negotiate.

THE RELIGIOUS STRIFE THAT HAD PLAGUED EUROPE *since the Reformation climaxed in the horrors of the Thirty Years' War. Starting as a struggle between the Catholic Holy Roman emperor and his Protestant subjects, it quickly grew into a multinational struggle setting the Hapsburg emperor against foreign forces eager to tame his power. The chief losers were the people of the central European regions that served as battlegrounds; their populations were decimated and their lands laid waste.*

The first phase of the war began when the Hapsburg ruler Ferdinand II, an ardent Catholic who at the time was king of Bohemia and later became Holy Roman emperor, tried to impose anti-Protestant policies on his subjects. In protest, angry nobles threw two imperial counselors out of a high window in the Royal Palace in the "Defenestration of Prague." The rebels offered Elector Frederick V of the Rhenish Palatinate—a Calvinist—the crown, but his reign was brief; the so-called "Winter King" was defeated at the Battle of the White Mountain in 1620. Troops from Spain (also ruled by the Hapsburgs) occupied the Palatinate, and Bohemia was forcibly re-Catholicized.

Breaking a 12-year truce, Spain then moved to crush the enduring revolt against its rule in the Netherlands. To defend Dutch and north German Protestants, Denmark invaded Lower Saxony in 1625;

but its armies were repulsed, and it withdrew from the conflict four years later. By 1629 the forces of Catholicism were dominant, and in that year Ferdinand further tightened his grip with the Edict of Restitution, which deprived Protestants of hard-won freedoms held for over 70 years.

Yet at the very height of Catholic supremacy the tide started to turn. Splits arose within the imperial camp—even many Catholic princes suspected Ferdinand of

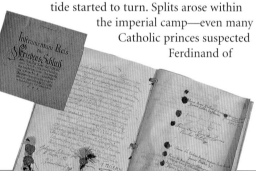

⚔ **1618** Two imperial counselors are thrown from a window of Hradcany Castle in Prague; the Bohemian–Palatinate War begins.

♛ **1619** Ferdinand II, the repressive ruler of Bohemia whose actions sparked revolt, is elected Holy Roman emperor in Vienna; a Protestant siege of Vienna fails.

⚔ **1620** Imperial forces under Johann Tilly triumph over Protestant champion Frederick V at the Battle of the White Mountain; Spain conquers the Rhenish Palatinate.

⚔ **1621** Under its new ruler Philip IV Spain breaks its 1609 truce with the Netherlands and invades to restore Catholicism.

♛ **1624** Cardinal Richelieu is appointed first minister in France by Louis XIII.

⚔ **1625** King Christian IV of Denmark joins the Protestant Union and invades northern Germany.

⚔ **1626** Danish forces suffer a heavy defeat by armies of the Catholic League commanded by Tilly and Wallenstein at the Battle of Lutter, near Hamelin, Lower Saxony.

⚔ **1628** Wallenstein unsuccessfully besieges the key Baltic port of Stralsund to disrupt trade between the chief Protestant allies, the Netherlands, Denmark, and Sweden.

☀ **1629** Ferdinand II's Edict of Restitution curtails Protestant freedom of worship and restores Catholic church estates in northern Germany.

♛ **1630** Following an electoral meeting (assembly of princes) at Ratisbon, Wallenstein is dismissed as commander of the imperial forces.

⚔ **1630** Gustavus II Adolphus of Sweden becomes the new champion of the Protestant cause, landing in Pomerania and advancing south almost to Vienna.

⚔ **1631** Besieged by Tilly, the city of Magdeburg capitulates, and its citizens are massacred. At the Battle of Breitenfeld in Saxony–Anhalt the Swedes and Saxons win a major victory over the forces of the Catholic League.

⚔ **1632** Wallenstein is restored as imperial commander; Gustavus II Adolphus is killed at the inconclusive Battle of Lützen.

Legend:
- ☐ Austrian Hapsburg territory 1618
- ▨ Spanish Hapsburg territory 1618
- ▨ German Protestant states 1618
- ▨ United Provinces 1618
- — borders 1648

0 — 300 km
0 — 200 mi

✕ major battle
→ French campaign
→ Hapsburg campaign
→ Protestant campaign
→ Swedish campaign

trying to extend his absolute power. The year 1630 marked a watershed when the emperor's ambitions were checked by his own allies at a meeting of German princes at Ratisbon. Meanwhile a new player's entry into the war tipped the military balance against the Hapsburg ruler. Under its dynamic king Gustavus Adolphus Sweden won a series of victories and advanced deep into southern Germany. Yet Swedish momentum faltered when Gustavus fell in the Battle of Lützen in 1632, followed by a defeat at Nördlingen (1634). Civilian casualties continued to mount; in the siege of Magdeburg an imperial army slaughtered almost all the city's 25,000 inhabitants.

An unlikely new ally of Protestantism now emerged in the form of Catholic France. To curb the power of the Holy Roman Empire, France's chief minister, Cardinal Richelieu, formed an alliance with anti-Hapsburg forces in 1635. Although French and Swedish armies made gains against the Spanish and imperial forces, neither side could win supremacy. When the moderate Ferdinand III succeeded to the imperial throne in 1637, the war entered a decade of bloody stalemate. Finally, in 1648, with the land exhausted by decades of bloodshed, an uneasy peace was concluded at the Treaty of Westphalia.

◀ The main theaters of conflict were in what are now southern and eastern Germany, Poland, and the Czech Republic, but fighting also spread into Italy, Austria, Denmark, and the Netherlands.

Wallenstein

The most charismatic military leader of the Thirty Years' War was Albrecht von Wallenstein. Brought up as a Protestant in Bohemia, he converted to Catholicism in 1606 and won distinction at the Battle of the White Mountain in 1620 (right). Amassing great wealth by confiscating Protestant noblemen's property, Wallenstein raised an army of 24,000 men for the imperial cause. Appointed supreme commander, he led his troops to victory over Danish forces in north Germany from 1624 to 1629. His success won him enemies, however, and the emperor was forced to dismiss him in 1630. Recalled two years later to counter the Swedish threat, he regained Bohemia but failed to achieve a decisive breakthrough. After a second dismissal in 1634 Wallenstein was accused of treason by Ferdinand II and murdered by British mercenaries.

🏛 **1635** The Peace of Prague brings the conflict between the Holy Roman Empire and Saxony to an end; Cardinal Richelieu of France forms an alliance with Sweden.

✕ **1635** A long war of attrition breaks out between France and Spain; France seizes Martinique and Guadeloupe in the Caribbean from the Spanish (–1648).

✕ **1648** The Thirty Year's War is ended by the Peace of Westphalia. The power of the Hapsburgs is checked, and religious freedoms within Germany are reaffirmed.

17

AMERICAS

⊛ **1630** The city of Boston is founded.

✗ **1630** Dutch forces make their first attempt to conquer northeastern Brazil but are soon driven out by the Portuguese.

♕ **1632** French settlers found Acadia (modern Nova Scotia, Canada).

⊛ **1634** Searching for a northwest passage to Asia, French explorer Jean Nicolet crosses Lake Michigan.

♕ **1635** The French occupy and colonize the Caribbean islands of Martinique and Guadeloupe.

EUROPE

⊛ **1630** An outbreak of bubonic plague causes 500,000 deaths in Venice.

♕ **1630** At the Ratisbon electoral meeting (assembly of princes) Holy Roman Emperor Ferdinand II dismisses Albrecht von Wallenstein as supreme commander of the imperial armies.

✗ **1630** Swedish forces under King Gustavus II Adolphus intervene in the Thirty Years' War to aid the Protestant cause and invade northern Germany.

✗ **1631** Following the Siege of Magdeburg by imperial (Catholic) forces under Count Johann Tilly, the victorious army sacks the city and slaughters most of its 25,000 inhabitants.

✗ **1632** King Gustavus II Adolphus of Sweden is killed leading his troops at the Battle of Lützen (Saxony).

☀ **1633** Galileo Galilei is forced by the Inquisition to recant his view that the sun is at the center of the universe; he is subsequently put under house arrest and banned from studying the heavens.

📖 **1634** The Académie Française, an organization fostering France's cultural heritage and the French language, is founded by Cardinal Richelieu in Paris.

♕ **1634** Branded a traitor by the emperor, Wallenstein is murdered by English mercenaries in Eger, Hungary.

⊛ **1637** "Tulipmania" reaches its height in the Netherlands, with one speculator swapping a house in Haarlem for just three bulbs; prices will eventually crash by 95 percent.

AFRICA

♕ **c. 1630** Ife is eclipsed as the dominant Yoruba state in what is now Nigeria by the rise of the Kingdom of Oyo.

✗ **1637** Elmina, a key Portuguese trading port on West Africa's Gold Coast, is captured by the Dutch.

WESTERN ASIA

✗ **1630** Ottoman Sultan Murad IV captures the Persian city of Hamadan.

Sultan Murad IV, ruler of the Ottoman Empire.

✗ **1638** After a month-long siege Ottoman forces recapture Baghdad from the Persian Safavids; Iraq becomes an Ottoman province until 1918.

SOUTH & CENTRAL ASIA

📖 **1632** Following the death of his wife Mumtaz Mahal, Mughal Emperor Shah Jahan orders the construction of her tomb, the Taj Mahal at Agra, which will take 22 years to complete.

✗ **1632** Shah Jahan embarks on the conquest of the Deccan (central India); at the same time, a famine in the region causes one million deaths, with cannibalism rife.

✗ **1634** Shah Jahan drives the Uzbeks from Kandahar in Afghanistan.

⊛ **1639** The English East India Company founds a trading base at Fort St. George (modern Madras) on the southeastern coast of India.

EAST ASIA & OCEANIA

♕ **1634** Ligdan Khan, last ruler of the Great Khanate of Mongolia (originally established in 1206), dies, and the Manchus overrun the region.

♕ **1636** In Mukden, northeastern China, the Manchus proclaim the Qing Dynasty. The Ming Dynasty holds onto power in the rest of China, although in a weakened state.

♕ **1636** As part of a campaign to eradicate Western influence in Japan, all foreigners are forced to live on the artificial island of Dejima in Nagasaki harbor.

📖 **1636** Harvard University, the oldest university in the United States, is founded in New Towne (later Cambridge), near Boston, Massachusetts.

✗ **1637** Conflict breaks out between New England settlers and the indigenous Pequots, resulting in hundreds of deaths on both sides.

⊛ **1638** The first printing press in North America is set up by Stephen Day in Cambridge, Massachusetts.

"I think, therefore I am," wrote the French thinker René Descartes, outlining the first step in a rationalist worldview that has led him to be called the father of modern philosophy. In his *Discourse on Method* and other works he laid out the basis of a system of thought that in future decades would come to underpin the scientific revolution. A practicing Catholic, Descartes nonetheless advocated the questioning of all established beliefs in an attempt to create a universal scheme of knowledge founded on mathematical standards of proof. The emphasis that he placed on the exercise of reason challenged the medieval notion of discovering truth through faith and prepared the way for a newly critical approach to intellectual activity.

👑 **1637** Emperor Ferdinand II dies in Vienna and is succeeded by his son Ferdinand III.

⊛ **1637** In his *Discourse on Method* French philosopher René Descartes proposes his principle of methodical doubt whereby science begins with observation, followed by analysis.

☀ **1638** Scottish Presbyterians sign the National Covenant, opposing the divine right of kings and English interference in Scottish Protestant affairs.

⊛ **1638** Firmly established at St. Louis on the Senegal River, French settlers begin to paticipate in the transatlantic slave trade.

👑 **1639** Shah Safi of Persia and Murad IV sign the Treaty of Qasr-i-Shirin, which establishes a permanent border between their empires.

📖 **1639** Shah Jahan orders construction of the walled city of Old Delhi. He will move the Mughal capital there nine years later (−1648).

The Taj Mahal, built as a mausoleum for the wife of Shah Jahan.

✗ **1637** Japan's Shogun Iemitsu crushes a Christian peasant uprising in the Shimabara region. Iemitsu's forces capture Hara Castle and massacre its defenders (−1638).

⊛ **1639** Russian explorers reach the Pacific coast of Siberia.

👑 **1639** Portuguese traders are expelled from Japan.

👑 **1639** All Japanese ports except Nagasaki (used by Dutch merchants) are closed to trade with the outside world.

AMERICAS

EUROPE

AFRICA

WESTERN ASIA

SOUTH & CENTRAL ASIA

EAST ASIA & OCEANIA

1630–1640 A.D.

19

JAPAN CLOSES ITS DOORS

▲ A European trader as seen by a Japanese artist.

▼ Tokugawa power in Japan spread out from a base on the central island of Honshu.

*J*APAN WAS FIRST EXPOSED TO WESTERN INFLUENCE *in the middle of the 16th century. Long accustomed to prosperous trade with China, the Japanese initially welcomed the growth in commerce stimulated by European merchants. Yet Japan was a country of strict social divisions and longstanding religious traditions, and its rulers soon reacted strongly against the activities of Christian missionaries. Fearing that European nations had colonial ambitions, Japan closed its doors on foreigners in 1641; over two centuries were to pass before they opened again.*

As a result of the conquests of Toyotomi Hideyoshi (1536–1598) Japan had become steadily more unified and stable before the Tokugawa Dynasty took control of the shogunate in 1603. Peace brought with it greater opportunities for trade, for the development of industry and agriculture, and for improved communications and transport.

Trade with China, which had been going on for a thousand years, grew considerably, with local feudal warlords adopting Chinese culture as a sign of their new respectability. As the 16th century went on,

however, another entirely unfamiliar influence—that of Europe—made its mark on Japanese society.

The first contact with Europeans happened by chance when a Chinese ship with two Portuguese travelers on board was shipwrecked off Tanegashima in 1542. Significantly, the foreigners sold their muskets to a local lord; soon replicated by the Japanese, these firearms transformed warfare there and played a vital role in the country's unification under strong military leaders.

The Portuguese seaborne empire, pushing ever farther east, began regular trade with Japan in 1570 with the opening of the port of Nagasaki to foreign commerce. The Japanese viewed the Europeans with cautious openness; after the English explorer Will Adams was shipwrecked on Kyushu in 1600, he served the ruling strongman Ieyasu, who became shogun three years later, as an adviser. Adams (who

Legend:
- Tokugawa domain 1560–89
- Japan under the Tokugawa Bakufu from 1603
- Nagasaki — port remaining open to foreign trade after 1641
- important city or town
- castle town
- "Five Highways" of Tokugawa Japan

0   300 km
0   200 mi

Hokkaido
Hakodate
Matsumae
Miyuma
Hirosaki   Hachinohe
Noshiro
Akita   Miyako
Ichinoseki
Sakata
Sado   Yamagata   Sendai / Shiroishi
Niigata
Nagaoka   Aizu
Shirakawa   Iwaki
Kanazawa   Toyama *Honshu* Utsunomiya
Oki   **JAPAN**   Takasaki   *Tone*
Fukui   Choshi
Sabae   Edo (Tokyo)
Matsue   Tottori   Obama   Iida   Odawara   Kanagawa
Fushima   Nagoya   Uraga
Hamada   Kyoto   Sumpu   Shimoda
Tsushima   Hagi   Hiroshima   Hyogo   Osaka
Fuchu   Yamaguchi   Wakayama   Toba   *Izu Islands*
Akamagaseki   Matsuyama   *Shikoku*   Tanabe
Hirado   Kochi   Oshima
Goto Islands   Funai   Uwajima
Nagasaki   Shimabara
Shimo   *Kyushu*   Nobeoka
Kagoshima   Miyazaki

KOREA Manchu vassal since 1637

Sea of Japan

PACIFIC OCEAN

Tanegashima first Portuguese traders arrive 1542
Osumi Islands

☸ **1542**   Portuguese travelers make a first, accidental landfall in Japan following a shipwreck off the southern tip of Kyushu.

☀ **1548**   A missionary expedition led by the Jesuit Francis Xavier travels to the Japanese capital of Kyoto and to Kagoshima in western Japan to win converts to Christianity (–1551).

☸ **1570**   The southern port of Nagasaki is opened to foreign trade.

☀ **1587**   Japan's Shogun Hideyoshi bans Christianity and expels Jesuits from the country.

♛ **1598**   The death of Hideyoshi leaves a power vacuum, plunging the country into civil war.

took the Japanese name of Miura Anjin) won permission for Dutch and English traders to operate in Japan and also developed Japan's own merchant fleet. The commodities the foreign merchants sought were gold, silver, and copper from new mines. They exchanged the metals for raw silk and finished textiles brought from China as well as new types of firearms.

Relations with the foreigners, however, soon worsened over the question of religion. Jesuit missionaries from Spain and Portugal arrived in the wake of the traders, converting many Japanese, particularly among the influential feudal daimyo (lords). Along with Christianity they brought new

technical knowledge, for example in mathematics, astronomy, engineering, and mining. But their influence came to be bitterly resented by enemies who suspected them of destabilizing the country in preparation for foreign invasion. A long series of persecutions followed. The final impetus for the expulsion of the Europeans and their religion came with the Shimabara Rebellion of 1637, after which Japan retreated into two centuries of isolation.

▼ A Japanese painting shows a Portuguese sea captain watching his men disembark on an early visit to the country. Europeans were at first welcomed as curiosities but were later expelled.

The Massacre at Hara Castle

A major uprising against Tokugawa rule broke out in December 1637 on the Shimabara Peninsula near Nagasaki. It was sparked by the levying of heavy taxes on the peasant population. The area had been Christianized in around 1612, and the repeated torture and murder of converts had fueled discontent. Under their young, charismatic leader Amakusa Shiro the rebels occupied Hara Castle and held out for three months against a large force sent to quell them. Yet starvation and overwhelming odds finally brought defeat. All 37,000 defenders were slaughtered; some 11,000 were beheaded, while others were burned alive. Archaeological excavation of the site, which began in 1992, has uncovered several small crucifixes, rosaries, and icons of Christ, the Virgin Mary, and the missionary leader Saint Francis Xavier.

⚔ **1600** At the Battle of Sekigahara the warlord Tokugawa Ieyasu defeats three rivals to win undisputed control over Japan.

👑 **1603** After being awarded the hereditary title of shogun (military dictator) by the emperor, Tokugawa Ieyasu moves the seat of government to Edo (present-day Tokyo).

✳ **1609** Breaking the Portuguese monopoly on trade with Japan, the Dutch East India Company establishes a base on Hirado Island near Nagoya at the invitation of the shogun.

☀ **1612** Ieyasu begins his persecution of Christians in Japan, particularly local converts to the faith.

✳ **1613** The first English trading mission opens in Hirado; it will be abandoned in 1623.

⚔ **1615** Ieyasu mounts a major operation against Osaka Castle, a stronghold of opposition to his rule under the control of Hideyori, Hideyoshi's only surviving son.

✳ **1616** The shogun's English adviser Will Adams helps the Japanese build ocean-going vessels and sails to Siam to expand trade links.

👑 **1616** Ieyasu dies, to be succeeded by his son Tokugawa Hidetada.

👑 **1623** Hidetada abdicates in favor of his 19-year-old son Iemitsu.

👑 **1633** Decrees ban Japanese, on pain of death, from trading or living overseas (–1635).

⚔ **1638** A Christian-led revolt on the Shimabara Peninsula near Nagasaki is put down brutally.

👑 **1639** Portuguese traders are expelled from Japan. Two years later the Dutch—the only remaining Europeans—are restricted to the artificial island of Dejima.

AMERICAS

✕ **1640** Violent conflict flares in Brazil as Jesuit priests attempt to prevent the enslavement of the indigenous peoples by Portuguese colonists.

👑 **1641** The General Court of Massachusetts Bay Colony sets out the Body of Liberties, a code of 100 laws that includes the legalization of slavery.

👑 **1642** French settlers found a colony at Ville de Marie in Canada, later to be called Montreal.

EUROPE

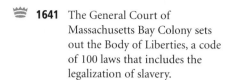

✕ **1640** Catalans revolt against the centralizing policies of Philip IV's chief minister, the Count–Duke of Olivares.

✕ **1640** Portuguese forces take advantage of the Catalan revolt to win freedom from Spanish rule. John of Braganza becomes king.

✕ **1642** In the Thirty Years' War Swedish forces defeat imperial troops in the Second Battle of Breitenfeld.

The Count–Duke of Olivares, Spain's chief minister, as painted by Diego Velázquez.

✕ **1643** A Baltic war breaks out between Sweden and Denmark.

👑 **1643** Philip IV's hated righthand man, the Count–Duke of Olivares, falls from power.

✕ **1644** Under pressure from Oliver Cromwell England's Parliament forms the New Model Army to fight the civil war against King Charles I; the army is commanded by Sir Thomas Fairfax, with Cromwell as his second-in-command.

AFRICA

✕ **1641** Dutch forces take Luanda, capital of Angola colony, from the Portuguese. They will hold it for the next seven years.

👑 **1641** Garcia II becomes king of Kongo (Zaire).

WESTERN ASIA

👑 **1640** Ottoman Sultan Murad IV dies and is succeeded—disastrously— by his son Ibrahim the Mad.

Ottoman Sultan Ibrahim the Mad, deposed and killed in 1648.

✕ **1642** With the help of Crimean Tatars Ottoman forces drive the Cossacks from Azov, a setback for Russian ambitions on the Black Sea coast.

SOUTH & CENTRAL ASIA

⊛ **1641** The English East India Company establishes a trading base at the river port of Hooghly in Bengal, downstream from modern Calcutta.

✕ **1641** Russian forces begin an 11-year campaign to subdue the Buryat Mongols of the Baikal region, Siberia (–1652).

✕ **1642** Gushri Khan, ruler of the Qosot Mongols, conquers Tibet and installs the fifth Dalai Lama, Ngawang Lobsang Gyatso, in Lhasa as ruler of what will from now on be a theocratic state.

EAST ASIA & OCEANIA

✕ **1641** The Dutch capture of Malacca underlines their dominance throughout the East Indies.

👑 **1641** Safiyat ud Din Taj ul-Alam comes to the throne of Aceh, beginning half a century of female rule in the Indonesian sultanate.

👑 **1641** Japanese authorities move Dutch merchants from Hirado to the island of Dejima in Nagasaki harbor for closer supervision.

👑 **1642** In Cambodia King Chetta II's son Chan takes power after a bloody palace coup.

⊛ **1642** Dutch navigator Abel Tasman becomes the first European to sight Van Diemen's Land (later Tasmania) and New Zealand.

⊛ **1644** Russian forces reach the Amur Valley of eastern Siberia.

🏛 **1643** Connecticut, Massachusetts Bay, Plymouth, and New Haven colonies come together in the New England Confederation, a defensive alliance.

✕ **1644** A Native American uprising around Jamestown, Virginia, kills 400 colonists.

☀ **1648** A book by Miguel Sanchez hailing the apparition of the Virgin of Guadalupe, Mexico City, launches the greatest Catholic cult in the Americas.

England's long list of kings and queens runs back for more than a thousand years with just one gap—the 11-year period known as the Interregnum between the execution of the deposed King Charles I in 1649 and the crowning of his son Charles II in 1660. The nation was ruled for most of this time by Oliver Cromwell, leader of the victorious parliamentary armies in the preceding civil war—his sword hilt is shown at left. Taking the title of lord protector, he proved a competent, dedicated leader who enforced order at home and raised the country's prestige abroad. But the harsh Puritanism of his regime roused hostility, and within two years of his death in 1658 leading figures in the kingdom had determined that England's future well-being would best be served by the restoration of the monarchy.

☀ **1647** George Fox founds the Society of Friends ("Quakers") in England.

✕ **1648** The Treaty of Westphalia brings the Thirty Years' War to an end, guaranteeing independence for the Dutch Republic, the Swiss Confederation, and some 250 German states.

🏛 **1649** A new law code restricts the rights of Russia's serfs (peasants) to such an extent that they can be bought and sold as slaves.

🏛 **1643** The French establish the colony of Fort Dauphin in southwestern Madagascar.

⊕ **1645** The first slaves are exported from Mozambique to Brazil.

☀ **1648** Portuguese Jesuits and other western missionaries are expelled from Ethiopia for interference in the country's religious affairs.

🏛 **1642** The Safavid Shah Safi of Persia dies; he is succeeded by his son Shah Abbas II, whose reign will be characterized by a new mood of religious intolerance.

✕ **1648** Shah Abbas II takes Kandahar, Afghanistan, from the Mughals.

🏛 **1648** Sultan Ibrahim is executed at the prompting of his own Janissaries.

✕ **1646** Mughal forces embark on what will turn out to be an ill-advised campaign in Central Asia.

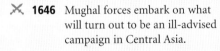

The Potala Palace rises majestically over the Tibetan capital of Lhasa.

🏛 **1646** Amangkurat I inherits the throne of Java. His tyrannical reign begins with mass executions of potential opponents and religious scholars; some 6,000 people are killed in the first year.

⊕ **1647** The first English colony in Myanmar (Burma) is founded at Syriam. Ten years later it will be abandoned, unable to contend in a region dominated by the Dutch, by that time at war with England.

⊕ **1648** Russian explorer Semyon Dezhnyov leads an expedition along the Arctic coast and around Asia's northeast cape (now Cape Dezhnyov) to the Pacific.

AMERICAS
EUROPE
AFRICA
WESTERN ASIA
SOUTH & CENTRAL ASIA
EAST ASIA & OCEANIA

1640–1650 A.D.

THE MANCHUS IN CHINA

THE NOMADS OF THE NORTHERN STEPPE *exerted an influence on Chinese history over many centuries, their lifestyle despised, their incursions deeply feared. These rootless raiders were an alien presence against whom the Chinese defined themselves as a settled, civilized, industrious, and peaceful people. Yet there were times when the nomads came to the rescue of the culture that so reviled them; the accession to power of the Manchu Qing Dynasty was one such occasion.*

▲ To Confucian intellectuals of the Ming Dynasty the Manchus were barbarians who could in no way match their own sophisticated culture, symbolized by the exquisite vase above. But the northerners took advantage of spreading disaffection to impose their rule.

The Juchen, or Manchus, a tribal grouping from the lands to the north of China, had already established a solid power base before they overthrew China's Ming Dynasty, having earlier united Manchuria under their rule and also won victories over the Mongols and Koreans. Their attention was inevitably drawn to the rich lands to the south, where growing economic disarray and political disaffection were causing a

breakdown in order. In the early 1640s rebellion spread through much of the country, forcing the last Ming emperor to the dangerous expedient of inviting the disciplined and efficient northern forces to shore up his rule. The request came too late to save his throne; the rebels reached Beijing in 1644, and the ruler himself committed suicide. The Manchu army took advantage of the power vacuum that ensued to

▶ A contemporary painting shows Emperor Kangxi entering a Chinese town on a tour through his realm in 1699. By that time the ruler had already reigned for 37 years, but he still had more than two decades of power ahead of him.

🜲 **1644** The Ming Dynasty collapses; the Manchu regent Dorgon declares that his protégé, the five-year-old Emperor Shunzi, has initiated a new imperial dynasty, the Qing.

🜲 **1645** An imperial decree proclaims that all Chinese must shave their foreheads and wear their hair in a long plait in the Manchu style.

🜲 **1650** Death of Dorgon.

⚔ **1659** The last Ming holdouts on the Chinese mainland finally fall to Manchu forces.

🜲 **1662** Emperor Kangxi comes to the throne at the age of seven, assisted by regents; he grants his Chinese subjects parity with the Manchus.

⚔ **1667** The imperial regent Obei seizes power in a palace coup. Two years later the emperor reasserts his authority, and Obei is killed.

⚔ **1673** The Revolt of the Three Feudatories breaks out (–1681) in southern China, led by rebellious generals.

🜲 **1673** Emperor Kangxi embarks on a series of imperial tours to inspect his realms.

🜲 **1683** The Qing Empire annexes Taiwan.

🜲 **1722** Emperor Kangxi dies.

seize power in the Manchus' own name. Their leader Dorgon became the true ruler of China, although technically only as a regent for his five-year-old nephew, who took the regnal name of Shunzi, first emperor of China's new Qing, or "pure," Dynasty.

The man who did most to impose the authority of the Qing was Shunzi's successor Kangxi, who came to power at the age of seven on Shunzi's death in 1662. At first the empire was run by regents, but Kangxi disposed of the last of these in 1669, taking power in his own name at the age of just 15.

Kangxi proved in every way an exceptional ruler. A man of immense energy and intellectual curiosity, he set out to accomplish a delicate balancing act, winning the support of the native Chinese for the new dynasty without alienating the Manchu warriors who had put it in power. At first he had to cope with armed resistance, especially in the south, and in 1673 trouble broke out again when three generals who had been appointed provincial governors sought to break away in the Revolt of the Three Feudatories.

Kangxi overcame these challenges to his rule by adopting a carrot-and-stick approach, on the one hand inaugurating important programs of public works, restoring canals, and building flood defenses, while on the other clamping down hard on dissent and disorder. The emperor also succeeded in developing a power structure in which native Chinese subjects could rise to high office, and the traditional Confucian values of the empire's civil service were maintained. Kangxi lived on until 1722, bequeathing to his successors an empire basking in a golden age of peace and prosperity.

▶ The Manchus rose to power by expanding from a small homeland north of the Korean Peninsula to take control first of Manchuria and Inner Mongolia and then of China itself.

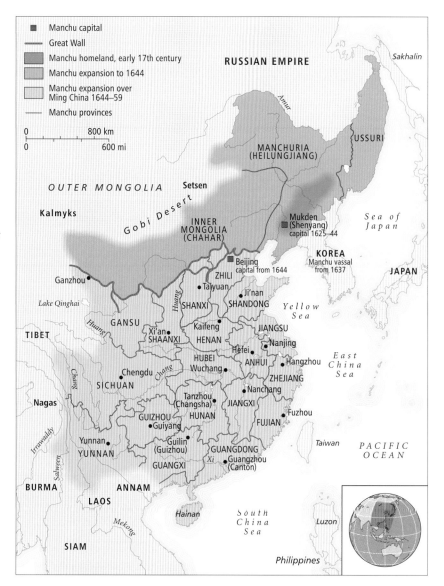

The Imperial Palace at Shenyang

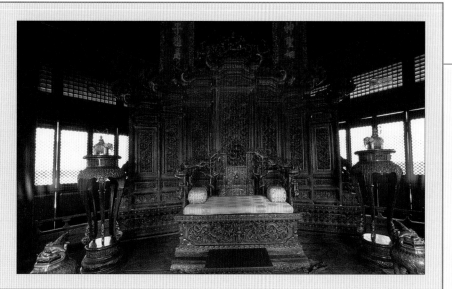

The Imperial Palace at Shenyang (or Mukden, as the Manchus called it) was built by the Manchu emperors shortly before they conquered the rest of China and established the Qing Dynasty. The building lies in Liaoning, now a northeastern province of China but at that time an outlying territory that had recently been conquered by the nomads. Construction began under Nurhachi in 1625 and was completed by his successor Abahai 11 years later. The palace was built as a replica of the famous Forbidden City in Beijing, although only about one-tenth its size, and was intended from the start as a statement of the Manchus' ambitions to rival or supplant the declining Ming Dynasty. It remained in use as an imperial summer palace throughout the centuries of Qing rule, serving as a constant reminder to the emperors of their Manchurian roots.

1650–1660 A.D.

AMERICAS

1654 The Dutch West India Company gives up its attempt to suppress a Portuguese settlers' revolt in Brazil.

1655 Peter Stuyvesant, the Dutch governor of New Netherland (New York and New Jersey), expels the Swedish colonists of New Sweden (Delaware).

EUROPE

1651 England introduces the first of a series of protectionist Navigation Acts: All trade from its colonies must be carried in English vessels.

Dutch and English fleets confront one another in the course of the First Anglo-Dutch War.

1652 The Dutch Republic declares war on England in response to the Navigation Laws, starting the First Anglo-Dutch War (–1654).

AFRICA

1650 Dombo Changamire conquers the Torwa Kingdom in Zimbabwe, establishing the Rozwi Dynasty.

1650 Portuguese forces complete the recapture of Angola from the Dutch.

1651 English settlers establish Fort St. James at the mouth of the Gambia River as a base for trade inland.

A 17th-century book illustration depicts inhabitants of the island of Zanzibar, off the coast of East Africa.

WESTERN ASIA

1650 Muscat is taken from the Portuguese by Sultan bin Saif al-Yarubi of Oman.

1656 The appointment of Mehmed Kiuprili as Ottoman grand vizier brings stability after a period of near anarchy.

1658 Abaza Hashan Pasha leads a revolt in Anatolia. It will be put down by Mehmed Kiuprili the following year.

SOUTH & CENTRAL ASIA

1656 Dutch forces take the city of Colombo in Ceylon (Sri Lanka) from Portugal. Over the next two years they will seize the island's other Portuguese colonies.

1658 Fort St. George, the future Madras, becomes the overall headquarters of East India Company operations in India.

1658 The Mughal Emperor Shah Jahan is deposed and imprisoned by his son Aurangzeb. The new emperor will seek to enforce strict Sunni orthodoxy, repressing Sikhism and Hinduism along with minority Islamic groups.

1658 After 20 years of struggle the Dutch win the coastal region of Sri Lanka from the Portuguese, although the inland Kingdom of Kandy remains an independent state.

1659 Sivaji, a Marathan Hindu warlord from southwest India, takes the city of Bijapur from the Mughals.

EAST ASIA & OCEANIA

1651 Japan's Shogun Iemitsu dies, and Ietsuna succeeds to the Tokugawa shogunate. He puts down two coup attempts in his first two years and is then secure.

1652 The king of Tran Ninh's refusal to wed his daughter to his neighbor King Souligna Vongsa of Laos triggers an invasion, his forced compliance to the match, and the start of a 200-year feud.

1656 Narai becomes king of Ayutthaya (Siam). His 32-year reign will be marked by commercial and cultural openness to the outside world.

✗ **1655** England takes Jamaica from Spain.

⊕ **1658** French traders Médard Chouart des Grosseilliers and Pierre-Esprit Radisson explore territories to the west of Lake Superior.

☀ **1659** Fray García San Francisco y Zuniga establishes the mission that will form the nucleus of the city of El Paso.

AMERICAS

✗ **1652** Barcelona surrenders to Philip IV of Spain, bringing the Catalan Revolt to an end.

✗ **1654** Ukrainian Cossacks rise against Polish rule, offering their allegiance to Czar Alexis I and sparking a 13-year war that will end with Russia taking Ukraine.

✗ **1655** The First Northern War breaks out when Charles X of Sweden declares war on Poland.

✗ **1656** A Swedish victory at the Battle of Warsaw sparks declarations of war from Russia, Denmark, and the Holy Roman Empire.

✗ **1656** Britain joins France in a war against Spain.

✗ **1658** Anglo–French forces defeat the Spanish at the Battle of the Dunes. England gains Dunkirk.

👑 **1658** Leopold I is enthroned as Holy Roman emperor.

👑 **1659** The Treaty of the Pyrenees is signed by Spain and France, which makes territorial gains. The treaty marks the end of the Spanish ascendancy in Europe.

EUROPE

✗ **1652** Omani Arabs capture Zanzibar from Portugal; a 70-year struggle begins for control of East Africa's Swahili Coast.

👑 **1652** Dutch settlers found a colony at Cape Town, South Africa.

⊕ **1659** French merchants build a new, larger base at St. Louis on the Senegal River that will become the main French trading post in West Africa.

✗ **1659** Ottoman janissaries based in Algiers revolt, appointing their own *agha*, or commanding officer, as governor.

👑 **1659** The last Saadi sultan of Morocco is assassinated in Marrakech.

AFRICA

✗ **1658** The Ottomans begin a lengthy siege of Candia, the capital of Crete.

WESTERN ASIA

Known as the "World-holder," Aurangzeb was the last of the great Mughal emperors, noted as much for his religious zeal and building activities (at right, the Badshahi Mosque in Lahore) as for his military campaigns. In the course of a 48-year reign he pushed the boundaries of the empire to their greatest extent, but at a cost—his lengthy wars in the Deccan exhausted the imperial treasury. Meanwhile his intolerance of all faiths but the Sunni version of Islam alienated numbers of his subjects and built up future opposition to Mughal rule.

SOUTH & CENTRAL ASIA

👑 **1658** Cambodian princes depose Chan with the help of forces from Hué, which exacts pledges of loyalty and tribute in return.

👑 **1659** Yungli, the last serious Ming pretender to the throne of China, takes refuge in Burmese territory. His hosts are forced to return him four years later, and he is publicly executed.

✗ **1659** The Chinese rebel leader Zheng Chenggong, known in the West as Coxinga, fails in an attempt to sieze the city of Nanking from the country's new Manchu rulers.

EAST ASIA & OCEANIA

1650–1660 A.D.

ENGLAND'S REVOLUTION

▲ Charles I holds the royal scepter and a model church in a statue symbolizing his status as head of the Church of England, a role that antagonized his many Puritan opponents.

IN THE MID-17TH CENTURY two concepts of sovereignty came into bloody conflict in England. On one side stood King Charles I of the Stuart Dynasty, a conscientious but blinkered ruler with an unshakeable belief in the "divine right of kings" to govern as they saw fit. On the other was the country's Parliament, representing the property-owning upper classes, who were equally convinced that they had a right to a say in the way the nation was run. The result was civil war.

Charles I was unpopular with his Parliament from the outset: They suspected him of covert Catholic leanings, and he made no secret of his belief in his god-given right to rule as he pleased. They knew that he would do without them if he could, and from 1629 he did precisely that, for 11 years. Matters came to a head in 1640 when Charles was forced to recall parliament by shortage of money: He needed new taxes approved to wage the "Bishops' War," fought to force the Scots to accept the authority of the Anglican church. This policy was as unacceptable to English Puritans as it was to the Presbyterian Scots: Both were equally hostile to the established church hierarchy.

This first parliament proved uncooperative, so after 23 days Charles dissolved it and called another. This "Long Parliament"—with interruptions it sat for 20 years—exacted concessions in return for qualified support. The compromise proved inadequate to a deteriorating situation. Early in 1642 Charles invaded Parliament with 400 soldiers, hoping to arrest five radical members, only to find, in his words, that "the birds had flown." His heavy-handed action alienated moderate opinion, and both sides prepared for war.

The Royalist forces had the best of the opening exchanges, since the Parliamentarians had to build their own army from scratch. But Charles proved indecisive while his enemy was getting better organized all the time. The Parliamentarians found a military leader of genius in Oliver Cromwell, who fashioned an instrument to win the war in the "New

---

👑 **1625** Charles I becomes king of England on the death of his father James I.

👑 **1629** Charles dismisses Parliament, starting an 11-year period of personal rule.

👑 **1640** Charles summons, then promptly dissolves, the "Short Parliament."

👑 **1640** The "Long Parliament" gets under way.

⚔ **1642** Civil war breaks out between Royalists and Parliamentarians.

⚔ **1644** Cromwell's New Model Army defeats Royalist forces at the Battle of Marston Moor.

⚔ **1645** Parliamentary forces decisively defeat the Royalists at Naseby.

👑 **1646** Charles surrenders to the Scots.

Condemned to Death

Repeatedly defeated, Charles I gave himself up to the Scots army in England in 1646. The Scots handed Charles over to the English Parliamentarians but later fell out with them and with the leadership of the English army. In 1648 the Scots unsuccessfully invaded England on Charles's behalf, but were heavily defeated. The English army went on to purge Parliament and put Charles on trial for treason. The king defended himself stoutly, but the verdict was never in doubt. His death warrant (below), specifying that the king should be "put to death by the severing of his head from his body," had no fewer than 59 signatories (Cromwell's name comes third from the top in the lefthand column). Charles went to his death on January 30, 1649, wearing two shirts so that he should not be seen to shiver in the cold morning air. He won more support by his death than he had enjoyed in his life. Public opinion across the nation was shocked by the execution, and his persecutors had difficulty in establishing the legitimacy of their rule.

Model Army," a dedicated force that was strengthened in its resolve by the Puritan views of many of its soldiers. (Popularly they were known as "Roundheads," their hair being cropped far shorter than the flowing locks of the royalist Cavaliers.) They won at Marston Moor and then, decisively, at Naseby.

Defeated in battle, the king sought sanctuary with the Scots. Their loyalties were divided: Charles had been no friend to them, so they handed him over to the English. But when Charles escaped from captivity and the Scots fell out with the English Parliamentarians, they sent an army to invade England in his name. This force was defeated. The king, who had meanwhile been recaptured, was put on trial in London in 1649 and beheaded.

The Parliamentary victors then set about founding a republican "commonwealth," but it proved inherently unstable. Cromwell cut through the constitutional arguments to provide decisive rule; but when in 1653 he dissolved Parliament just as Charles had done, taking for himself the title of "lord protector," people came to the conclusion that they had merely exchanged one dictator for another. On his death in 1658 there was little appetite to replace him. Two years later Charles's son Charles II was invited back to England, and the monarchy was restored, although with additional safeguards against absolutism. England's revolution had come to an end.

▲ A crude woodblock illustration dating from 1649 shows Charles's execution, which took place in London before a huge crowd.

▼ Parliamentary forces held London throughout the war, gradually driving back the Royalists to the farthest parts of Britain.

1647 The Scots hand Charles over to the English Parliament. He escapes and makes a secret treaty with the Scots.

1648 A Scottish army invades England but is turned back at Preston. Charles is captured once again.

1649 Charles is tried and executed; England becomes a republican commonwealth.

1650 Charles's son, the future Charles II, lands in Scotland and is proclaimed king. Invading England, he is defeated at Worcester and flees to France.

1653 Cromwell dissolves Parliament and takes power as lord protector.

1658 Cromwell dies, succeeded as lord protector by his son Richard.

1659 "Tumbledown Dick" Cromwell is removed from office by the army.

1660 The Restoration sees the monarchy restored in the person of Charles II.

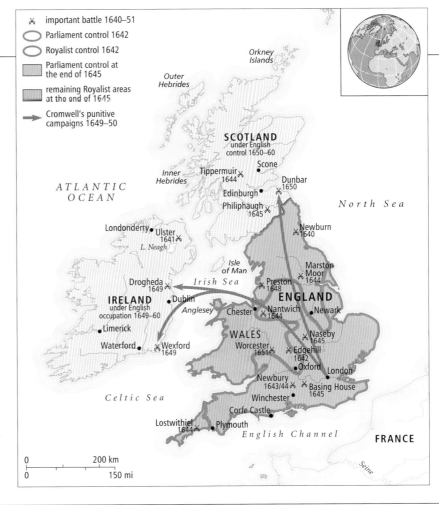

1660–1670 A.D.

AMERICAS

1661 The Dutch West India Company formally renounces its interest in Brazil.

1662 Slavery is authorized in the English colony of Virginia.

1663 King Charles II of England grants a royal charter to the proprietors of the Carolina colony. Four years later he also grants them rights over the Bahama Islands.

1664 English forces take New Amsterdam from the Dutch. Fearing annexation by the newcomers, the colony of New Haven unites with Connecticut.

EUROPE

1663 An Ottoman army is turned back in the Alps at St. Gothard, an apparent triumph for European power, but the Ottoman Empire comes off best in the ensuing negotiations.

1665 The Second Anglo-Dutch War breaks out, with the Dutch supported by France and Denmark. The English win an initial victory over a Dutch fleet off Lowestoft.

1665 The Great Plague breaks out in London. Over the next 18 months it will claim 68,500 lives in England.

1665 Philip IV of Spain dies and is succeeded by the sickly Charles II.

1666 The Great Fire of London destroys over 13,000 houses and almost 90 churches.

1666 Reforms in the Russian Orthodox church lead to the defection of the conservative Old Believers.

1667 The Dutch defeat an English fleet at the Battle of the Medway River.

1667 The Treaty of Breda brings peace between the Dutch Republic, England, France, and Denmark.

1667 The Russo–Polish war ends with the Treaty of Andrussovo.

AFRICA

c.1660 In response to growing Western influence Islamic leader Nasir al-Din launches a *jihad* (holy war) in the kingdoms of northern Senegambia (between the Senegal and Gambia rivers).

Mulay Rashid, sultan of Morocco.

1661 Garcia II dies and is succeeded as king of Kongo by Antonio I. The kingdom is coming under increasing pressure from Portuguese forces based in the colony of Angola to the south.

WESTERN ASIA

1661 The Ottoman Grand Vizier Mehmed Kiuprili dies, to be succeeded by his son, starting a dynastic tradition in the post that will survive for more than a century.

1664 After their defeat at the Battle of St. Gothard the Ottomans salvage their authority in the Peace of Vasvar, concluded on favorable terms with the Austrians thanks to the Kiuprilis' diplomatic skills.

1665 Shabbetai Tzevi, the "False Messiah," proclaims his messianic mission. His claims are dismissed by rabbis but euphorically embraced by ordinary Jews throughout the Diaspora.

SOUTH & CENTRAL ASIA

1662 Mughal forces of the Emperor Aurangzeb conquer Assam, although they will be forced out again four years later.

1664 The Mughal armies continue their conquests in northeast India by taking Bengal.

1664 Sivaji sacks Surat: He is beginning to carve out a Marathan Hindu kingdom in the southern Deccan.

1666 The deposed Mughal Emperor Shah Jahan dies in prison in Agra.

EAST ASIA & OCEANIA

1662 Dutch forces drive the Spanish from the Moluccas.

1662 The Chinese rebel leader Zheng Chenggong (Coxinga) establishes a new base on Taiwan, taking control of the island from the Dutch.

1663 Spanish settlers abandon their fort at Zamboanga and with it their interest as a colonial power in the southern Philippines.

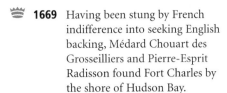
🏛 **1665** French Jesuit Claude Jean Allouez founds the Chequamagon Bay Mission on Lake Superior's Wisconsin shore.

🏛 **1669** Having been stung by French indifference into seeking English backing, Médard Chouart des Grosseilliers and Pierre-Esprit Radisson found Fort Charles by the shore of Hudson Bay.

✴ **1669** René-Robert Cavelier, sieur de La Salle, sets out from Montreal to explore areas south of Lakes Ontario and Erie.

AMERICAS

As the photograph suggests, the *starovery*, or Old Believers, remain a presence in Russia to this day. The movement had its origins in the 1660s, when the patriarch of the Russian Orthodox church announced sweeping liturgical reforms that conservatives within the church refused to accept. Breaking away, they formed their own schismatic movement, which subsequently split into a number of different sects. The Old Believers, who remain deeply traditional in their views, suffered persecution for the first two centuries of their existence but won official recognition from 1871 on.

EUROPE

✴ **1663** An English trading post is established in Sierra Leone, West Africa.

🏛 **1664** Mulay Rashid becomes ruler of the Alawid clan of southern Morocco.

⚔ **1665** Antonio I is killed by the Portuguese at the Battle of Mbwila. Kongo begins to disintegrate.

🏛 **1666** Mulay Rashid takes Fez from Morocco's ruling Saadi Dynasty, now in steep decline, and establishes his capital there.

🏛 **1667** King Fasilides of Ethiopia dies, to be succeeded by his son John I.

AFRICA

🏛 **1666** Safavid Shah Abbas II dies, but the persecution of non-Muslims in Persia continues under his son Shah Sulayman.

Memorial shrine in the house of the "False Messiah" Shabbetai Tzevi in Izmir, Turkey.

⚔ **1668** Ottoman forces capture Basra on the southern coast of Iraq; the rule of the Afrasiyab Dynasty in the city is overthrown.

⚔ **1669** Ottoman forces finally take Candia, and with it all Crete, from the Venetians.

✴ **1668** The English East India Company is granted land for a colony at Bombay (Mumbai).

☀ **1669** Aurangzeb outlaws Hindu worship in India, a major step in enforcing an increasingly intolerant Sunni Islamic state.

WESTERN ASIA

SOUTH & CENTRAL ASIA

🏛 **1664** Siam (modern Thailand) is forced into signing a treaty giving the Dutch a monopoly on its foreign trade.

⚔ **1666** Mughal forces take the Burmese port of Chittagong.

☀ **1668** The Spanish Jesuit Diego Luis de San Vitores establishes a mission on Guam in the Mariana Islands.

EAST ASIA & OCEANIA

FRANCE'S SUN KING

▲ The sun radiates in majesty above the Earth on a silver medallion coined in Louis XIV's time. France's all-powerful monarch delighted in solar imagery, seeing the splendor of his own rule as an earthly reflection of the sun's heavenly glory.

LOUIS XIV HIMSELF BEST SUMMED UP *his constitutional position in France when he proclaimed, "L'Etat, c'est moi" ("I am the State"). For much of his 73-year reign it seemed just so: France reached a zenith under the Sun King, emerging as Europe's preeminent power and eclipsing such earlier rivals as England and Spain. Yet there was a downside to Louis's rule: The cost of his endless wars overtaxed the treasury, and his absolutism eventually paved the way for the French Revolution.*

Few would have guessed when Louis XIV became king of France in 1643 that he was destined to be the dominant figure of his age. He was only five years old at the time and seemed an insignificant figure beside his capable regent Cardinal Mazarin, who quickly stamped his mark on an office he filled with energy and autocratic arrogance. Thanks to Mazarin's deft diplomatic footwork, the Treaty of Westphalia concluding the Thirty Years' War proved a triumph for France, now a leading actor on the European stage. At home, though, Mazarin came to be hated. Hunger and high taxes alienated the common people, while his high-handed treatment of the nobility provoked a bitter and protracted series of revolts, collectively known as the Fronde, against his rule.

Louis only emerged as a dominant figure in his own right on Mazarin's death in 1661. The expected announcement of a new chief minister never came; instead, Louis assembled a team of exceptional talents that were to serve him well over the ensuing decades.

These men included the Marquis de Louvois, who became minister of war; the engineer Vauban, famed for his defensive fortresses; and above all, Jean-Baptiste Colbert, controller of France's finances for over 20 years. The main goals the young king set himself were to tame the fractious aristocracy that had so troubled Mazarin and to replace the Hapsburg rulers of the Holy Roman Empire and Spain as Europe's most powerful monarch.

Louis's marriage to Maria Teresa, the heiress to the Spanish crown, gave him the perfect lever with which to chip away at Spanish power. Nominally his queen had given up all claim to the Spanish throne in exchange for the payment of a huge dowry, but Louis was able to use bankrupt Spain's inability to come up with the money as a pretext for war. France's early successes against the Spanish Netherlands alarmed not only the neighboring Dutch Republic but also the two main northern European powers, England and Sweden. Together they formed the Triple Alliance,

---

👑 **1643** Louis XIV becomes king of France at the age of five.

👑 **1648** The Treaty of Westphalia concludes the Thirty Years' War: The setbacks the settlement represents for Hapsburg Spain and the Holy Roman Empire are a boost for France.

⚔ **1648** The Fronde (literally "catapult") breaks out—a five-year series of revolts against the crown (–1653).

👑 **1659** France's chief minister, Cardinal Mazarin, brokers the Treaty of the Pyrenees. Louis agrees to wed the Spanish Infanta (crown princess) Maria Teresa, who renounces her claims to the Spanish throne in exchange for the payment of a large dowry by Spain.

👑 **1661** Cardinal Mazarin dies; Louis XIV makes himself absolute monarch.

⚔ **1667** The War of Devolution begins with a French invasion of the Spanish Netherlands, claimed by Louis on behalf of his queen.

⚔ **1668** The Triple Alliance pits England, the Dutch Republic, and Sweden against France.

⚔ **1668** The War of Devolution comes to an end with the Treaty of Aix-la-Chapelle. France keeps most of its conquests in the Spanish Netherlands.

⚔ **1672** France goes to war with the Dutch, later joined by the Hapsburg emperor, from whom France makes sizable gains (–1678).

☀ **1685** Louis revokes the Edict of Nantes, which since 1598 has guaranteed the right of France's Protestant Huguenots to worship freely.

⚔ **1688** Louis invades Protestant states of Germany, initiating the War of the League of Augsburg (–1697).

⚔ **1701** The War of the Spanish Succession begins.

⚔ **1713** The Treaty of Utrecht resolves the Spanish succession issue in favor of Louis's grandson Philip, but France loses territories in the Americas and along its own northeastern frontier.

👑 **1715** Louis XIV dies and is succeeded by his son Louis XV.

France on accession of Louis XIV 1643
permanent gains during the reign of Louis XIV 1643–1715
Réunions of Louis 1684–97
other temporary gains under Louis XIV
■ new town established
□ new fort established
■ major port development
— boundary of France 1715

North Sea

ENGLAND

UNITED PROVINCES

English Channel

HOLY ROMAN EMPIRE

Dunkirk to England 1658–62
FLANDERS
Lille
ARTOIS
Meuse
Rhine

Le Havre
Caen
Rouen
Luxembourg
Longwy
Sarrelouis
Metz
Mont Royal
Fort Louis
Versailles
Paris
Seine
Nancy
ALSACE
Strasbourg
Neuf Brisach
LORRAINE

Brest

Lorient

Orléans
Loire
Tours
Nantes
Richelieu
Henrichemont
Bourges
Besançon
FRANCHE-COMTÉ
Rhine
Huningue

CHAROLAIS
SWISS CONFEDERATION

ATLANTIC OCEAN

Rochefort
Limoges
FRANCE
Lyon
Rhône
SAVOY-PIEDMONT

Bordeaux
Pinerolo
Mont Dauphine
GENOA

Montauban
Avignon to the Papacy
Bayonne
Toulouse
Sète
Canal du Midi built 1664–84
Marseille
Toulon

SPAIN
Mont-Louis

0   300 km
0   200 mi

which successfully checked further French expansion, although France was able to hold onto most of the conquests it had already made.

Subsequently Louis would fight three more wars against his European neighbors. The urge to defend Catholicism was a growing theme of his policy, and it also led him to launch a crackdown on France's own Protestant minority, the Huguenots. Although French armies for the most part held their own, the cost of taking on much of Europe exhausted the royal treasury and caused widespread economic hardship at home. By the later years of Louis's reign France's cultural preeminence was unchallenged, but its people were increasingly discontented, and the growing autocracy and religious intolerance of his rule had helped sow the seeds of the French Revolution.

◀ Louis XIV fought four major wars in his long reign, at first making substantial territorial gains, especially in the north and east. By the time of his death, however, his forces were overstretched and his people overtaxed, and some of the newly won lands were lost as rival powers allied to counter French might.

▼ The formality of Versailles's design was matched by the ordered ceremonial of the court life played out within its corridors and halls. Louis consciously set out to tame France's aristocracy by insisting that nobles spend most of their time at court, occupied in an unending theater of status and display.

Versailles

Louis XIV's self-promotion transcended mere vanity; he made no distinction between his own personal glory and that of the country he ruled. It seemed no more than fitting, then, that in 1668 he should give orders for a splendid palace to be built outside Paris at Versailles. Designed by Louis Le Vau and Jules Hardouin-Mansart, the edifice was conceived as a showcase for French wealth and power. The finished building was stunning in its magnificence and in its sheer scale, its western facade alone measuring 1,900 feet (580 m) long. Inside the palace hundreds of rooms were decorated with all the opulence appropriate to the royal residence of the greatest monarch of the age. Outside, in the ornamental gardens laid out by André le Nôtre, fountains played among spacious avenues and secluded walks.

AMERICAS

✕ **1670** The English pirate Henry Morgan captures Panama.

👑 **1670** English forces take possession of the Caribbean island of Jamaica.

✴ **1671** Two Englishmen, Batts and Fallam, are the first Europeans to cross the Appalachian Mountains.

☀ **1671** The Pope canonizes the first New World saint, Rose of Lima, the daughter of Spanish settlers in Peru who became a nun.

✴ **1673** French explorers Father Jacques Marquette and Louis Joliet reach the headwaters of the Mississippi River.

✴ **1674** Jacques Marquette founds a mission on the shores of Lake Michigan; it will become the city of Chicago.

👑 **1674** The Treaty of Westminster confirms the English possession of New Amsterdam; it is renamed New York.

✕ **1675** King Philip's War breaks out when native Americans under Metacomet (King Philip), chief of the Wampanoags, rise up against the colonists of New England. The rising is put down, but not before one in 16 of all adult male settlers in the region has been killed (–1676).

✴ **1679** The French begin to explore the upper Great Lakes and discover Niagara Falls.

EUROPE

Calculating machine devised by the French thinker Blaise Pascal.

👑 **1670** By the Treaty of Dover, a secret agreement with Louis XIV, Charles II of England deserts the Triple Alliance and ends hostilities with France.

📖 **1670** The *Pensées* of Blaise Pascal, French mathematician and religious thinker, are published eight years after his death.

✕ **1672** The army of Louis XIV of France invades the Netherlands.

✕ **1674** William of Orange, leader of the Dutch Republic, floods low-lying coastal land in Holland to halt the French advance.

AFRICA

👑 **c. 1670** The Lunda Empire of central Africa extends its grip to the upper Zambezi River region.

👑 **c.1670** The Ashanti are by now beginning to emerge as a powerful state in West Africa.

👑 **1672** Mulay Ismail succeeds Mulay Rashid as sultan of Morocco.

WESTERN ASIA

✕ **1672** The Ottoman Empire goes to war with Poland, winning Podolia and parts of Polish Ukraine (–1676).

📖 **1673** French traveler Jean Chardin visits Esfahan on a great journey through Turkey and Persia.

✕ **1677** War breaks out between the Ottoman Empire and Russia following Cossack raids on Ottoman territory.

SOUTH & CENTRAL ASIA

👑 **1674** The French East India Company founds a base at Pondicherry, south of Madras in India.

👑 **1674** Sivaji, the leader of the Marathas of western India, has himself crowned as a Hindu king.

☀ **1675** Aurangzeb arrests and executes the Sikh guru Tegh Bahadur, who had refused to embrace Islam.

☀ **1675** Goband Singh becomes the last of the Ten Gurus of Sikhism and openly rebels against the Mughals.

📖 **1677** Jean Chardin reaches India on his travels, visiting the courts of the Mughals and the Deccani sultans before returning to Europe.

EAST ASIA & OCEANIA

✴ **1673** Mitsui Takatoshi of the Mitsui banking family opens a dry goods store in Edo, Japan; it is the predecessor of the celebrated Mitsukoshi department store.

👑 **1673** A French mission brings letters from the pope and King Louis XIV of France to the court of Siam (Thailand).

✕ **1673** The revolt of the Three Feudatories breaks out in China when Wu Sangui, governor of Yunnan and Guizhou provinces, refuses to accept an order to give up his office (–1681).

King Philip's War broke out in 1675 in response to settlers' encroachments on Native American lands in New England. Metacomet, known to the colonists as King Philip, led an alliance of the tribes living from Maine to Rhode Island in a ferocious campaign that took the insurgents within 20 miles (30 km) of Boston, attacking 52 of New England's 90 settlements and destroying 12 of them. Eventually the settlers' firepower told, and the war came to an end in 1676 with Metacomet's death. His wife and children were sold into slavery in the West Indies.

👑 **1675** John Sobieski is elected king of Poland.

✖ **1675** Louis XIV's General Turenne defeats the armies of Prussia and Austria at the Battle of Turkheim.

✖ **1675** The Swedes invade Brandenburg–Prussia in support of the French but are decisively beaten at the Battle of Fehrbellin.

⚙ **1676** The Royal Observatory is founded in London, England.

👑 **1676** Fyodor III becomes czar of Russia.

📖 **1678** English Puritan writer John Bunyan publishes *The Pilgrim's Progress*.

👑 **1678** By the Treaties of Nijmegen concluding the Dutch War Louis XIV gains valuable territories in the north and east of France; he is now the most powerful ruler in Europe (–1679).

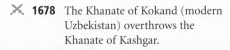

Kara Mustafa, Ottoman grand vizier from 1678 until 1683.

✖ **1677** The French capture Dutch trading posts on the coast of Senegal.

👑 **1678** Kara Mustafa, a brother-in-law of Ahmed Kiuprili, becomes grand vizier and effective ruler of the Ottoman Empire.

✖ **1679** Aurangzeb seizes the Rajput Kingdom of Marwar.

👑 **1679** Aurangzeb restores the *jiziya* tax levied by the Mughals on non-Muslims.

✖ **1678** The Khanate of Kokand (modern Uzbekistan) overthrows the Khanate of Kashgar.

✖ **1679** Galdan, ruler of the Oirat and Zunghar Mongols, conquers much of present-day Xinjiang province with the help of the Dalai Lama.

Shanhaiguan Castle in northern China, held by Wu Sangui at the time of the Manchu takeover.

AMERICAS

EUROPE

AFRICA

WESTERN ASIA

SOUTH & CENTRAL ASIA

EAST ASIA & OCEANIA

1670–1680 A.D.

THE DUTCH REPUBLIC

The STORY OF THE DUTCH REPUBLIC *is one of determination, enterprise, and good fortune. By the mid 17th century this small country on the coast of northern Europe, still less than 50 years old, had become the most powerful trading nation in the world. Dutch ships sailed far and wide, carrying grain and timber from the Baltic to France and Spain and bringing spices and luxury goods from Southeast Asia to Europe. As Dutch merchants and traders grew rich and prosperous, the country enjoyed a golden age of art and science.*

▲ A relief sculpture shows a Dutch warship of the type used to support the nation's far-flung mercantile interests. The prosperity of the Netherlands in the 17th century relied heavily on mastery of the sea.

▶ The Dutch trading empire had three main focuses. First and foremost came the Spice Islands of the Dutch East Indies, followed by trading posts on the Indian coast. The third area was the Caribbean, which supported a busy trade in sugar, tobacco, and slaves.

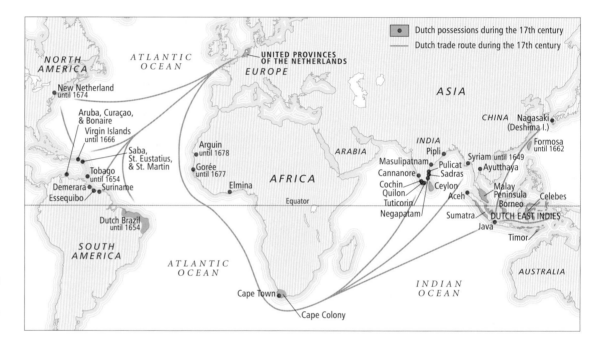

- Dutch possessions during the 17th century
- Dutch trade route during the 17th century

1588   The United Provinces become a republic, having won their freedom from Spain.

1602   The Dutch East India Company is founded to trade with Southeast Asia.

1609   The Amsterdam stock exchange is founded.

1619   The Dutch East India Company founds a trading station at Batavia (now Jakarta) on Java, which becomes the center of its Asian trading empire.

1629   French philosopher René Descartes settles in the Dutch Republic, remaining there until 1649.

1642   Rembrandt paints *The Nightwatch*.

1642   Dutch navigator Abel Tasman discovers Tasmania (which he calls Van Diemen's Land) and New Zealand.

1648   Spain formally recognizes the independence of the Dutch Republic in the Treaty of Westphalia.

1656   Christiaan Huygens builds a pendulum clock.

c.1660   The painter Jan Vermeer is at his peak, painting domestic interiors such as *The Girl with a Pearl Earring*.

1667   A Dutch fleet sails up England's Thames and Medway rivers and destroys the naval shipyards at Chatham during the Second Anglo-Dutch War.

1672   Louis XIV of France sends an army to invade the Netherlands. To halt its advance, the Dutch open the dykes and flood lowlying lands. In this crisis William III of Orange comes to power (–1678).

1677   William marries Mary, eldest daughter of James, duke of York (later James II of England).

1689   William accepts the throne of England and rules jointly with his wife.

In the mid-16th century the Netherlands were part of the Catholic Kingdom of Spain. Most Dutch people were Protestant, however, and also disliked paying high taxes to Spain, so they rebelled. At first the Spanish put down the revolt with great ferocity. But in 1579 seven northern provinces formed an alliance to continue the struggle, and in 1588 these United Provinces declared themselves a republic. Although Dutch independence had in practice been gained, Spain refused to recognize the republic as an independent state until 1648.

The Netherlands lay at the crossroads of European trade. When the Spanish-held port of Antwerp went into decline as a result of the Dutch revolt, the port of Amsterdam was ready to take over. Soon enterprising Dutch merchants had seized control of the profitable spice trade from Portugal. Industries such as sugar refining and shipbuilding added to the wealth of the young state, while its policy of religious tolerance encouraged refugees from all over Europe to settle in its towns. The newcomers brought valuable skills with them such as clock- and telescope-making. Meanwhile Dutch engineers increased the amount of agricultural land by developing windmills to pump water and create polders (areas of land reclaimed from the sea).

The republic's prosperity encouraged an artistic blossoming. To show off their wealth, rich merchants had portraits painted of themselves and their families, and decorated the walls of their new townhouses with landscapes and scenes of everyday life by artists such as Vermeer, de Hooch, Cuyp, and Frans Hals. The outstanding Dutch painter of the day was Rembrandt, whose self-portraits and pictures such as *The Nightwatch* and *The Anatomy Lesson* are among the world's great masterpieces.

The republic was governed by the States-General, a parliament representing all the provinces, but the most powerful official was the stadtholder (chief magistrate) of Holland, the richest province. In practice this office was almost always held by the princes of Orange, whose forebear, William the Silent, had led the Dutch revolt. In effect, the office became hereditary, and in time the stadtholder was recognized as the head of government. When, in 1689, William of Orange became king of England following the expulsion of James II, he effectively became ruler of both countries. Previously the Dutch and English had fought three wars for mastery of the sea, but in future the English would take the leading role in colonial trade, bringing the republic's great days to an end.

Tulipmania

It is rare for a flower to bring about financial ruin, but that is what happened to hundreds of Dutch investors when the demand for tulip bulbs reached a peak in the 1630s. The vibrant colors of the blooms, recently introduced into Europe from Turkey, made them highly popular with gardeners. The sandy soils of the Netherlands proved well suited to growing the bulbs, which quickly became a fashionable status item. Soon people proved willing to pay high prices to get hold of them. In 1636 tulips began to be traded on the stock exchange of several Dutch towns, and the fashion turned into a speculative boom. People mortgaged their houses, land, and even businesses in order to make a killing in the tulip market, and bulbs were sold and resold while they were still in the ground. But the craze could not last. A panic set in in 1637, and the market collapsed overnight, sweeping away fortunes in its wake.

◀ Painted in 1642 when the great Dutch painter Rembrandt was 36 years old, *The Nightwatch* was commissioned as a group portrait of a civic guard

AMERICAS

⚙ **1681** French explorer the sieur de La Salle travels down the Mississippi River to reach the sea (–1682).

☀ **1681** English Quaker William Penn founds a colony on an area of land extending west from the Delaware River; it will later become Pennsylvania.

⚔ **1683** Dutch and English pirates sack Veracruz, Mexico.

⚔ **1687** La Salle is murdered by mutineers while leading an expedition to explore the Mississippi Delta.

⚔ **1689** La Salle's colony on the coast of Texas is attacked and completely destroyed by Native Americans.

⚔ **1689** War between England and France in Europe spreads to North America as King William's War, the first of the French and Indian Wars, which set settlers from the two nations against one another.

EUROPE

👑 **1682** Louis XIV moves his court to the new palace of Versailles outside Paris.

⚔ **1683** The Polish King John Sobieski leads an army to the rescue of Vienna, which is under siege by an Ottoman army.

Shown here on an ivory vase decoration, John III Sobieski was a champion of the European struggle against the Ottoman Turks. Elected to the Polish throne in 1674, he made common cause with the Hapsburg ruler of Austria when Ottoman forces invaded his lands and, as commander of a combined Austrian and Polish army, raised the siege of Vienna. He subsequently joined the Holy League against the Turks, but his later attempts to detach Black Sea territories from the Ottoman Empire came to nothing.

AFRICA

⚙ **1681** The last dodo, a large flightless bird, is killed by sailors on the island of Mauritius.

👑 **1682** Isayu I becomes king of Ethiopia and begins to open the country to trade with European and Arab states.

The dodo, made extinct by overhunting.

WESTERN ASIA

👑 **1681** Ottoman Grand Vizier Kara Mustafa assembles a large army to invade central Europe.

👑 **1683** After the defeat of the Ottoman army at the gates of Vienna Kara Mustafa is beheaded on the orders of the sultan.

👑 **1687** Mehmed IV, known for his love of hunting, is deposed as Ottoman sultan and replaced by his younger brother, Suleiman II.

SOUTH & CENTRAL ASIA

👑 **1680** The Maratha leader Sivaji dies. Known as the Grand Rebel, he had succeeded in thwarting the Mughal ruler Aurangzeb by establishing an independent Hindu kingdom in the Deccan.

👑 **1681** Prince Akbar leads an unsuccessful revolt against his father Aurangzeb, for which he is exiled.

👑 **1685** Aurangzeb expels the English East India Company from its base at Surat in western India.

EAST ASIA & OCEANIA

👑 **1680** The first Portuguese governor is appointed to Macao on the coast of China.

⚔ **1683** The Chinese use their fleet to expel the warlords who have occupied Taiwan since 1662; for the first time the island comes under direct imperial administration.

👑 **1684** The Japanese chief minister Hotta Mastoshi is assassinated, leaving Shogun Sunayoshi without advisers; he imposes impractical reforms that create widespread hardship.

This painting by American artist Edward Hicks shows William Penn, the English Quaker leader and founder of Pennsylvania, signing a treaty with local Native Americans. Penn obtained the territory from King Charles II in repayment of a royal debt owed to his father. He established a constitution for the colony that guaranteed religious freedom, and he achieved lasting good relations with the neighboring Delaware tribes by insisting that the treaty obligations were rigorously observed.

AMERICAS

EUROPE

👑 **1684** Pope Innocent XI establishes the Holy League, an alliance of Poland, Venice, and Hapsburg Austria, to liberate Europe from Turkish rule.

☀ **1685** Louis XIV cancels the Edict of Nantes, ending toleration of French Huguenots; thousands flee to Protestant lands.

✕ **1687** The Venetians besiege Athens, Greece, during a war against the Turks. A stray shell ignites an ammunition dump inside the Parthenon, and the ancient Greek temple is badly damaged.

✕ **1688** The Holy League captures Belgrade (modern Serbia) from the Ottomans.

👑 **1688** James II of England is deposed for his Catholic views.

✕ **1689** England, the Netherlands, Spain, and other European nations ally against Louis XIV's France in the War of the League of Augsburg (–1697).

📖 **1689** English philosopher John Locke publishes *An Essay Concerning Human Understanding.*

AFRICA

👑 **1684** The English abandon Tangier, on the coast of North Africa, and it passes to Morocco.

✕ **1684** The French attack pirate bases on the North African coast.

✕ **1686** French settlers build a fort on the island of Madagascar, which they claim as a French possession.

☀ **1688** French Huguenot refugees arrive as settlers in the Dutch colony of South Africa.

WESTERN ASIA

👑 **1689** Suleiman II makes Mustafa Kiuprili his grand vizier; he begins to reform the Ottoman army and administration.

Ottoman Sultan Suleiman II, painted by an Italian artist.

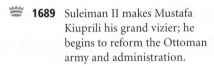

SOUTH & CENTRAL ASIA

✕ **1686** Aurangzeb conquers the Muslim Sultanate of Bijapur in the northwestern Deccan.

✕ **1687** Golconda, famous for its diamonds, falls to Aurangzeb.

✕ **1689** Sambhaji, Shivaji's son, is captured by a Mughal force; he is brought to Aurangzeb and executed.

EAST ASIA & OCEANIA

📖 **1684** The Japanese poet Saikuku composes 23,500 verses in 24 hours.

⊕ **1684** The Dutch East India Company occupies the Sultanate of Bantam on Java.

⊕ **1684** The English East India Company is granted permission to build a trading station at Canton (now Guangzhou) in southern China.

⊕ **1685** An English trading station is founded at Benkulen on the Indonesian island of Sumatra for the export of pepper.

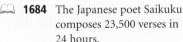

1680–1690 A.D.

RUSSIA'S DRIVE TO THE EAST

MOST PEOPLE HAVE HEARD OF *the great sailors such as Magellan, Tasman, and Cook who mapped the empty spaces of the Pacific Ocean, or of Lewis and Clark who made the first transcontinental crossing of North America. The story of the Russian pioneers who ventured overland across the vast expanses of Siberia to reach the Pacific Ocean is less well known, but it was filled with drama and excitement.*

Siberia stretches from the Ural Mountains in the west all the way across northern Asia to the Pacific Ocean in the east. The Arctic Ocean bounds it to the north and the mountains of Central Asia in the south. In between lie expanses of frozen tundra, vast forests, and swampy plains and lakelands, intersected at intervals by wide, northward-flowing rivers that empty into the Arctic Ocean.

Russians began to move beyond the Urals in the late 16th century. Encouraged by Czar Ivan the Terrible, a Cossack chief called Yermak Timofeyevich led an armed band of horsemen that in 1582 defeated Kuchum, the khan (ruler) of the local tribes, after a three-day battle. Yermak drowned soon after while crossing a river, dragged down, it was said, by his chainmail coat, a present from the czar.

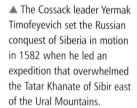

▲ The Cossack leader Yermak Timofeyevich set the Russian conquest of Siberia in motion in 1582 when he led an expedition that overwhelmed the Tatar Khanate of Sibir east of the Ural Mountains.

▶ Spectacular mountains like this peak near Petropavlovsk dot the Kamchatka Peninsula in the Russian far east, which has over a dozen active volcanoes. The first Russian to claim the peninsula was Vladimir Atlasov, who built two forts there in 1697.

👑 **1574** Ivan IV "the Terrible" grants the Stroganov merchant family land along the Tura and Tubol rivers east of the Ural Mountains.

⚔ **1582** Commissioned by the Stroganovs, the Cossack leader Yermak defeats Kuchum, khan of Sibir (a region of western Siberia), and captures his capital, Kashlyk.

⚔ **1587** A Russian fort is built at Tobolsk, not far from Kashlyk.

⚔ **1607** The Cossacks overcome resistance from the Tungus hunters of Siberia (–1610).

👑 **1632** Yakutsk is founded on the Lena River.

✳ **1639** The first Russians reach the Pacific Ocean.

✳ **1644** Vassili Poyarkov crosses the watershed from the Aldan to the Zeya River and reaches the Amur Basin.

⚔ **1648** A Russian fort is built on the upper Uda River beyond Lake Baikal.

✳ **1648** Semyon Dezhnyov sails through the Bering Strait.

✳ **1651** Yerofey Khabarov charts the Amur River (–1653).

👑 **1689** The Russians give up the Amur Basin by the Treaty of Nerchinsk.

👑 **1697** The Kamchatka Peninsula is claimed for Russia.

Semyon Dezhnyov, Arctic Explorer

Semyon Dezhnyov was a Cossack who made his way to northeast Siberia in search of furs and walrus tusks. In 1648 he led an expedition of about 100 men in seven small boats from the mouth of the Kolyma River on the Arctic coast eastward around the Chukotka Peninsula. Only three of the boats got as far as the entrance to the Bering Strait (later named Cape Dezhnyov), and only one made it all the way to the mouth of the Anadyr River. By making this perilous journey, Dezhnyov became the first person to show that the continents of Asia and North America were not joined. Some historians believe that the Dezhnyov expedition may have been the first to land in Alaska, but the theory remains unproven. It is known that Dezhnyov explored a number of islands in the Bering Strait and noted that the people inhabiting them decorated their lower lips with fragments of bone, stone, or walrus tusk.

Over the next century the Russians advanced rapidly. Most of the pioneers were Cossacks, warrior–adventurers from southern Russia. They traveled along the river systems in boats in the summer and in sleds when the steams were frozen in winter. As they advanced, they built fortified settlements where they could trade with local fur trappers, and each year a large consignment of the finest sables made its way back to the Russian court. They reached the Yenisey River by 1619 and the Lena River, where they founded the town of Yakutsk, by 1632. From there they made their way north to the Arctic Ocean. The first Russians reached the Sea of Okhotsk, an inlet of the Pacific, in about 1639. They founded the town of Anadyrsk on the Bering Sea and penetrated the mountainous Kamchatka Peninsula, Asia's northeasternmost point.

Meanwhile other explorers ventured south from Yakutsk. In 1643 Vassili Poyarkov led an expedition up the Aldan River to cross the mountains that divide Siberia from Outer Mongolia. His men reached the Amur River and journeyed down it to the Sea of Okhotsk, returning to Yakutsk in 1646. From 1651 to 1653 Yerofey Khabarov charted the length of the Amur River. A number of Russian forts were built along its banks, garrisoned by Cossacks who clashed with Chinese forces that were expanding into Mongolia from the south and considered the whole of the Amur Basin to be within their sphere of influence. At length the Russians agreed to abandon the forts. The Treaty of Nerchinsk (1689), which confirmed Chinese control over the Amur River, was the first treaty the Chinese ever made with a European power.

▶ An early print shows the city of Yakutsk, a Russian settlement in eastern Siberia built on the banks of the Lena River. The first fort was built there in 1632. Remote from other population centers and subject to extreme climate swings between winter and summer, the city served for centuries to harbor prisoners, political or otherwise, sentenced to internal exile.

▶ Russia's progress eastward across Siberia can be tracked by the new towns founded there in the 17th century. Most started out as forts or small fortified settlements.

new Russian town founded in the 17th century

Russian Empire at the start of the 17th century

Russian gains to 1689

0   1,600 km
0   1,000 mi

AMERICAS

1690 A Puritan force from Massachusetts lays unsuccessful siege to the city of Quebec during King William's War.

The arrest of a witch in 17th-century New England as imagined by the illustrator Howard Pyle.

1692 In Salem, Massachusetts, 19 women and girls are executed for witchcraft.

1692 Food shortages in Mexico City lead to the "Corn Riots," in which public buildings are burned.

1693 William and Mary College is founded in Williamsburg, Virginia.

EUROPE

1690 The clarinet is invented in Nuremberg, Germany.

1690 The Battle of the Boyne is fought in Ireland between England's deposed King James II, a Catholic, and his Protestant son-in-law and successor King William III. James's defeat ends his campaign to regain the English throne.

1694 François-Marie Arouet is born in France; he will become famous as the philosopher Voltaire.

1696 Peter the Great, czar of Russia, captures the important seaport of Azov near the mouth of the Don River from the Ottomans (–1698).

1697 Peter the Great makes a grand tour of Europe; traveling incognito, he visits shipyards in England and the Netherlands.

1697 Charles XII becomes king of Sweden at the age of 15.

1697 The Treaty of Ryswick ends the War of the League of Augsburg; all the towns and forts seized by Louis XIV since the Treaty of Nijmegen (1679) are to be handed back to their original owners.

AFRICA

c.1695 Isayu I of Ethiopia builds many churches in his capital Gondar, located north of Lake Tana.

1697 A French expedition led by André de Brue lays claim to Senegal in West Africa.

Church decorations in Gondar, Ethiopia.

WESTERN ASIA

1690 Mustafa Kiuprili organizes a large army that drives the Austrian army out of Serbia.

1691 Sultan Suleiman II is succeeded by his brother Ahmed II.

1691 Mustafa Kiuprili is killed fighting the Austrians at the Battle of Slankamen.

1694 Shah Suleiman of Persia dies and is succeeded by Shah Hussein.

SOUTH & CENTRAL ASIA

1690 Rajaram, Sambhaji's brother and successor as Maratha leader, is besieged in the great fortress of Senji by a Mughal army (–1698).

Matsuo Basho (1644–94), Japan's master of the three-line haiku poem.

1690 Job Charnock, chief agent for the English East India Company in Bengal, founds a trading station at Calcutta.

EAST ASIA & OCEANIA

1690 The Manchu court sends an army to defend the Mongols of Khalka (Outer Mongolia) against their neighbors, the Zunghars (West Mongols).

1694 Death of Matsuo Basho, considered the greatest of the Japanese *haiku* poets.

⊕ **c.1695** Gold deposits are discovered in Minas Gerais, Brazil, leading to a gold rush that attracts prospectors from Portugal.

⚔ **1697** King William's War between England and France ends with the English in possession of Port Royal (now in Nova Scotia).

⚔ **1697** The Spanish conquer Tayasal, capital of the last independent Maya state of Guatemala, which is located on an island in Lake Pétén Itzá.

⊕ **1698** The English Parliament passes the Woolens Act forbidding colonists in New England to ship wool or woolen products directly from one colony to another.

👑 **1699** The French colony of Louisiana is founded.

AMERICAS

⊕ **1698** English engineer Thomas Savery develops the first practical high-pressure steam engine for pumping water out of mines.

👑 **1699** The Ottomans cede most of Hungary to the Hapsburg rulers of Austria by the Treaty of Karlowitz, which concludes the war between Turkey and the Holy League and brings the era of

Charles XII of Sweden made his reputation as a military leader at the start of the Great Northern War, winning important victories over Danish, Saxon, and Russian forces. But an attempt to invade Russia in 1707 led to disastrous defeat at Poltava in 1709. Charles escaped to Ottoman territory in the Crimea, where he remained as a virtual prisoner for five years. He eventually returned to the Baltic region in 1714, spending the last years of his life in inconclusive military maneuvers before he was shot dead at a siege in Norway in 1718.

EUROPE

⚔ **1698** The Omani Arabs drive the Portuguese from their ports on the coast of East Africa and set up the Zanzibar Sultanate (–1700).

👑 **1699** Louis XIV of France sends an envoy to Ethiopia; he travels to Gondar overland from Egypt.

AFRICA

👑 **1695** Mustafa II succeeds Ahmed II as Ottoman sultan.

⚔ **1697** A Hapsburg force defeats an Ottoman army at the Battle of Zenta; the Turks lose nearly 30,000 men, along with huge quantities of supplies and ten of the sultan's wives.

WESTERN ASIA

⚔ **1693** The Dutch seize Pondicherry from the French and hold it until 1697.

☀ **1699** Goband Singh founds the Khalsa Brotherhood of the Sikhs. Khalsa means "pure."

A watercolor sketch by a Jesuit missionary shows the Dutch siege of Pondicherry in 1693.

SOUTH & CENTRAL ASIA

⚔ **1696** Chinese forces defeat a Zunghar army at Jao Modo in Outer Mongolia.

⚔ **1697** The Chinese overrun and occupy Outer Mongolia.

⊕ **1699** William Dampier becomes the first Englishman to land on Australia's west coast; he goes on to discover the Dampier Archipelago, named for him.

EAST ASIA & OCEANIA

1690–1700 A.D.

THE SCIENTIFIC REVOLUTION

WE TAKE IT FOR GRANTED THAT THE HEART *pumps blood around the body, that the planets orbit the sun, and that there are tiny organisms smaller than the human eye can see. Yet few people before 1600 would have believed any of these things. The situation had changed markedly by the end of the century, for enormous advances in knowledge had transformed understanding of the physical world. These advances are what historians describe as the scientific revolution of the 17th century.*

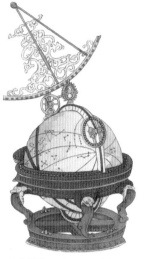

▲ A 17th-century astrolabe, used to measure the altitude of stars and planets.

Seventeenth-century Europeans were not the first people to study the nature of things. The Greeks had a great understanding of mathematics, astronomy, and the natural world; the Arabs studied medicine and mechanics. In early modern Europe, however, the Catholic church held that the Earth was the center of the universe as created by God, and that the universe was perfect and unchanging. This Bible-based view also accorded with the teachings of the fourth-century-B.C. Greek philosopher Aristotle. Anyone who challenged Aristotle's ideas therefore challenged the authority of the church.

Polish astronomer Nicolaus Copernicus used his knowledge of mathematics to calculate that the planets move around the sun rather than the sun around the Earth. He did not publish his ideas until 1543, when he was on his deathbed. It would be more than 60 years before anyone dared agree with him. Then, in 1609, the German astronomer Johannes Kepler argued that the planets moved in elliptical, rather than circular, orbits (an ellipse is a flattened oval), and in Italy Galileo used a telescope—a recent invention—to observe the heavens more closely than anyone had ever done before. He was the first person to see the mountains on the moon, the moons of Jupiter, the phases of Venus, and the spots on the sun. Galileo's observations led him to accept the Copernican system of a sun-centered universe.

Against the advice of friends he defended his ideas in a book published in 1632. The church immediately banned it and put Galileo on trial. Threatened with torture by the Inquisition, he recanted his views and was allowed to live under house arrest near Florence, where he carried on working until his death in 1642. Galileo's researches into mechanics and movement paved the way for the work of Isaac Newton, the

Large and Small

The discoveries of the scientific revolution would not have been possible without new instruments. A Dutch eyeglass-maker, Hans Lippershey, developed a telescope sometime before 1608; soon afterward Galileo Galilei used his own improved version to make revolutionary observations of the heavens. At the other end of the scale microscopes brought the world of the infinitesimally small into human view. Here again the pioneer was a Dutchman, Antoni van Leeuwenhoek, who used a lens he fashioned himself to study blood cells, fleas (right), and tiny bacteria. Another important invention was the airpump, which allowed Robert Boyle and others to investigate atmospheric gases.

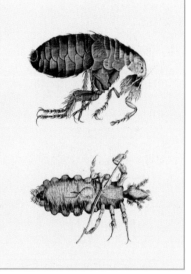

⊛ **1543** Nicolaus Copernicus argues that the sun is the center of the solar system.

⊛ **1543** Andreas Vesalius publishes the first modern anatomical text.

⊛ **1600** William Gilbert, in his work on magnets, deduces that the Earth itself acts as a magnet.

⊛ **1609** Johannes Kepler publishes his first two laws of planetary motion.

⊛ **1610** Galileo describes his astronomical observations with a telescope in *The Starry Messenger*.

⊛ **1628** William Harvey proves that the heart pumps blood around the body.

⊛ **1632** Galileo publishes his defense of the Copernican system.

⊛ **1644** Evangelista Torricelli describes a mercury barometer.

⊛ **1652** To demonstrate atmospheric pressure, Otto von Guericke pumps the air from two large metal hemispheres to create a vacuum; two teams of horses cannot pull them apart.

⊛ **1662** Robert Boyle establishes that the pressure and volume of a gas are inversely proportional.

⊛ **1662** The Royal Society of London is founded under the patronage of King Charles II.

greatest genius of the scientific revolution. Newton's experiments into the nature of light and his discovery of the laws of motion and gravitation were outstanding achievements that laid the foundations of modern physics.

In the 17th century the words "science" and "scientist" did not exist, nor were the new discoveries taught in universities. Groups of people interested in "natural philosophy," as it was called, formed academies or societies where they could meet to exchange ideas, discuss their experiments, and publish their results. One of the earliest of these bodies was the Academy of the Lynx, formed in Florence, Italy, in 1603. The Royal Society, founded in England in 1662, included among its early members such men as the architect Sir Christopher Wren, the microscopist Robert Hooke, the astronomer Edmond Halley, and Isaac Newton himself. These societies had enormous influence in helping to spread the new ideas of the scientific revolution.

▼ Scientists and doctors had had a clear idea of the anatomy of the human body since the 16th-century studies of Andreas Vesalius (below). The 17th century added a new understanding of its inner workings, especially the circulation of the blood.

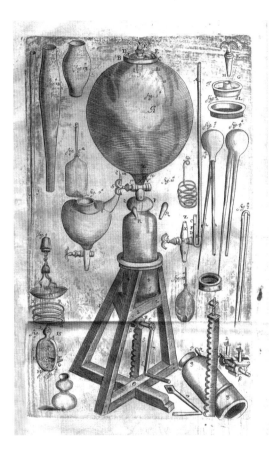

▲ An airpump devised by the English scientist Robert Boyle.

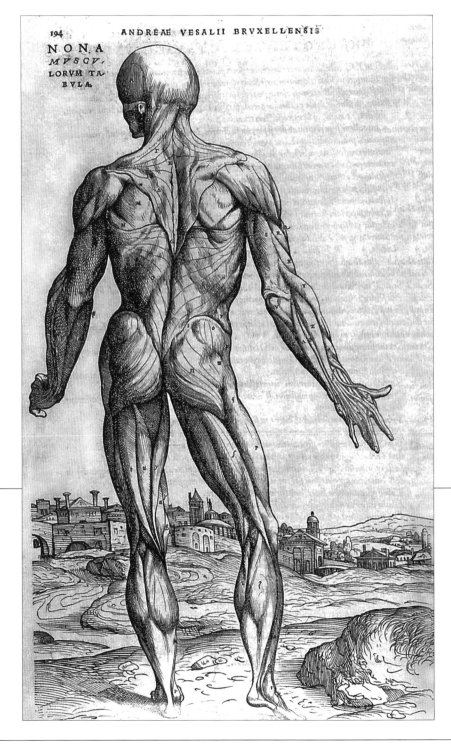

⚙ **1677** Antoni van Leeuwenhoek uses a microscope to examine male spermatozoa.

⚙ **1678** Christiaan Huygens proposes that light travels in waves.

⚙ **1687** Isaac Newton publishes *Principia Mathematica*, in which he sets out his three laws of motion.

FACTS AT A GLANCE

absolutism
An approach to government in which the authority of the ruler is total, with no restraining checks and balances.

Acadia
Province on Canada's Atlantic coast settled by France from 1632 but contested by the British, who called the region Nova Scotia (New Scotland). The British eventually secured the territory in the 18th century, deporting many of its French-speaking inhabitants to Louisiana, whose Cajun population derives its name from the word "Acadian."

Aceh, Sultanate of
Kingdom in northern Sumatra, Indonesia; the first Muslim stronghold in Southeast Asia, it reached its zenith under Sultan Iskander Muda (1607–1636). Aceh fiercely resisted Portuguese and later Dutch intervention in the region.

Afrasiyab Dynasty
A native of Basra in southern Iraq, Afrasiyab was awarded the governorship of that region in the 1590s. He went his own way, however, his successors continuing in power in what was increasingly an Ottoman province in name only.

agha
The title given to the officer in charge of a force of janissaries or slave-soldiers in the Ottoman Empire. Though himself a slave, he enjoyed considerable autonomy and power.

Akan
A group of peoples sharing the same language, the Akan originally lived in the savannah region inland of West Africa's Gold Coast but pushed south into the forest after gold and slaves. They became key trading partners of the Portuguese.

Algonquians
Indian peoples speaking related languages and inhabiting eastern Canada who allied with the French in the French and Indian Wars.

Anatolia
The Asiatic part of Turkey, known in Roman times as Asia Minor.

Angola
Portuguese colony established in lands south of the Congo River that had previously been a hunting ground for Kongo slavers who sold their captives to the Portuguese. By 1576, however, Portugal had its own coastal foothold at Luanda. The Dutch coveted the colony, seizing it briefly in the 1640s.

Aristotle
Greek philosopher (384–322 B.C.) who became tutor to Alexander the Great in 342. On returning to Athens, he set up his own school at the Lyceum.

Ashanti
After decades of war among the various Akan peoples, the Ashanti gained the ascendancy on Africa's Gold Coast. By 1700 their empire was the region's superpower, trading gold and slaves for the firearms that ensured its continuing dominance.

Assam
Independent state founded by the Ahom kings in the 13th century. After warring with Muslim Bengal in the 17th century, it was overrun by Burma from 1817 to 1822 and came under the control of the British Raj from 1826 on.

Ava, Kingdom of
Realm based near Mandalay, Upper Burma, which united the whole of the north of the country from 1368 on. The kings of Ava, half Burmese and half Shan, presided over a flowering of culture. Ava fell to the Mons in 1752.

Ayutthaya
Thai kingdom taking its name from its capital city, which rose to prominence in about 1350. After the capture of Angkor in 1431 Ayutthaya also ruled much of Cambodia. The realm was finally destroyed by the Burmese in 1767.

Azerbaijan
Territory on the western shore of the Caspian Sea. Conquered by Safavid Persia in the 1520s, it was contested by the Ottomans from the 1590s, but by 1618 the Safavids had regained possession.

Bantam, Sultanate of
Also known as Banten. Independent sultanate on Java. Following more than a century of European encroachment (thanks to its key position for the spice trade on the straits between Java and Sumatra), it was overrun by the Dutch in 1684.

Batavia
City on the northwestern coast of Java, Indonesia, known today as Jakarta. It was named by the Dutch when they seized it in 1619, making it the headquarters of the Dutch East India Company.

Bengal
Region in northeastern India annexed by the Mughal Empire in 1576. After the English founded Calcutta, Bengal came under the control of the East India Company. It is now divided between Bangladesh and the Indian state of West Bengal.

Bhutan, Kingdom of
Ancient kingdom in the eastern Himalayas long ruled by a spiritual figurehead, the Dharma Raja. Overrun by Manchu China from 1720 on, it increasingly came under the influence of the British Raj in India and was partly annexed in 1865.

Bijapur, Sultanate of
Region in south–central India, originally under the Bahmani Dynasty and later one of the Deccani Sultanates. It was conquered by Aurangzeb in 1686 and ceded to the Marathas in 1760.

Bishops' War
A rebellion (1639–1640) in Scotland following the decision of King Charles I of England and Scotland to impose bishops on the Presbyterian church in defiance of the National Covenant.

Body of Liberties
Compendium of laws created in Massachusetts Bay Colony in 1641 and often seen as a forerunner of the American Bill of Rights. The measures guaranteed limited religious toleration and the right to petition the government while banning "inhumane, barbarous, or cruel" punishments.

Bohemia
Part of the Czech Republic today, Bohemia was a medieval kingdom within the Holy Roman Empire with its capital at Prague. In 1526 it came under the rule of the Hapsburg Dynasty of Austria.

Brandenburg–Prussia
A state in northern Europe formed when the Hohenzollern family, hereditary electors (princes) of Brandenburg, acquired eastern Prussia through inheritance in 1618. Frederick William, the Great Elector (1620–1688), extended its boundaries even further by military conquest.

Buryat Mongols
Northernmost of the Mongol peoples, a nomadic and pastoralist group living south and west of Lake Baikal in Central Asia. Their territory was ceded to Russia by the Treaty of Nerchinsk (1689).

canonization
The process by which the Catholic church declares an individual to have been a saint.

cardinal
A high official of the Catholic church belonging to the Sacred College, from among whose number the pope is elected.

Carolina Colony
Colony established in North and South Carolina by settlers from Virginia in the mid-17th century and governed in the name of the British King Charles II (who gave the Latin version of his name, Carolus, to the territory).

cassava
Also known as "manioc," this crop was brought to Africa by the Portuguese from their Brazilian colonies. It can flourish in a wide range of soils and rainfalls, is easily propagated, and can be safely stored for long periods.

Catalan Revolt
A revolt (1640-1659) in Catalonia in northeastern Spain against the government of Olivares, chief minister of King Philip IV. The leaders of the revolt declared their independence from Spain and placed themselves under French protection.

charter
A legal document issued by a ruler or government conferring rights and privileges or establishing a constitution.

Commonwealth
The period of republican government in England from the execution of King Charles I in 1649 until 1660, when his son Charles II was restored to the throne.

Confucian
Pertaining to the celebrated Chinese administrator and philosopher Confucius (551–479 B.C.), known in China as Kongfuzi. In later times Confucianism, which emphasized learning, respect, and good conduct, became a state religion in China.

Copernican system
The theory that the sun is the center of the solar system and that the planets orbit around it, first outlined by the Polish astronomer Nicolaus Kopernik (Copernicus) in 1543.

Cossacks
Bands of warlike adventurers renowned for their horsemanship and courage, probably descended from peasants who had escaped serfdom to settle on the southern frontiers of Russia in the 14th century. They took part in the conquest of Siberia and were later recruited by the czars to form cavalry regiments in the Russian army.

Coxinga
(Zheng Chenggong; 1624–1662.) Ming pirate who harried the Manchu conquerors of China from the southern ports of Amoy and Quemoy. He led a major assault on Nanking in 1659 and seized the island of Taiwan from the Dutch in 1662.

Czar
The title of the ruler of Russia, derived from the Roman imperial title of caesar. It was adopted by Ivan IV the Terrible in 1547 and used by his successors until the Russian monarchy was abolished in 1917.

Dalai Lama
Spiritual leader of the dominant Yellow Hat sect of Buddhist monks in Tibet; the title was bestowed by the Mongol Emperor Altan Khan in c.1577. The fifth Dalai Lama (1617–1682) assumed secular authority and unified Tibet.

Deccan
An upland plateau occupying much of central and southern India, including inland areas of the modern states of Andhra Pradesh, Karnataka, Kerala, and Tamil Nadu.

Defenestration of Prague
Defenestration is the act of throwing someone out of a window. In 1618 Protestant nobles threw two imperial councillors from an upper window of Prague Castle and then elected the Protestant Frederick V of the Palatinate as king of Bohemia in place of the Catholic Holy Roman Emperor Ferdinand II—an act of rebellion that marked the start of the Thirty Years' War.

Dejima
An artificial island in Nagasaki harbor, Japan, to which Dutch merchants were confined (all other traders having been expelled) by order of Shogun Iemitsu after the Shimabara rebellion of 1637 and the subsequent persecution of Christians.

Denkyera, Kingdom of
Kingdom that arose among the Akan peoples of what is now southwest Ghana in the early 17th century.

diaspora
The dispersal of the Jews following the Roman sack of Jerusalem in 70 A.D. and the crushing of the Jewish revolt of 135.

divine right of kings
The belief that hereditary monarchs derive their authority to rule their subjects directly from God, from which it follows that rebellion against kings is disobedience to the will of God.

dowry
Goods, money, or land that a woman brings to her husband on marriage.

East India Company (Dutch)
Known in the Netherlands as the United East India Company (Vereenigde Oost-Indische Compagnie, or VOC), the Dutch East India Company was established in 1602 to exploit commerce with the East Indies. Headquartered at Batavia (modern Jakarta) on the Indonesian island of Java, it negotiated with (and sometimes fought against) local rulers, creating a virtual monopoly of the spice trade. The company fell into decline in the 18th century and went into liquidation in 1799.

East India Company (English)
English chartered company established in 1600, holding a trading monopoly on all commerce with the Indian subcontinent. It traded with the Mughal Empire and was engaged in a long struggle for supremacy with its French counterpart. It increasingly became an instrument of colonial administration until its sovereignty over India was finally transferred to the British crown in 1858 in the wake of the Indian Mutiny.

East India Company (French)
Trading organization founded in 1644 as a competitor to its Dutch and English counterparts. Establishing bases at Chandernagore and Pondicherry, its governor-general Joseph-François Dupleix vied unsuccessfully for power in India with the British in the mid 18th century. The company was dissolved in 1769.

Edict of Nantes
Order signed by King Henry IV of France in 1598 at Nantes, a city on the Loire River in western France, guaranteeing freedom of worship to Protestants. It marked the end of the French Wars of Religion, but was revoked by Louis XIV in 1685.

Edict of Restitution
An edict of the Holy Roman Emperor Ferdinand II, issued in 1629, decreeing that confiscated church property should be returned to whoever had possession of it in 1555—a measure aimed at recovering Catholic land lost to Protestants.

Elmina
Key Portuguese trading port on Africa's Gold Coast. The name is thought to be a corruption of a Portuguese term meaning "the mine."

Estates-General
The law-making body of France that met to advise the king. Made up of three estates, or assemblies, representing the clergy, nobility, and property-owning commoners, it was first summoned in 1302, but no assemblies were held between 1614 and 1789.

factory
A trading post of the English East India Company. The first was established at Surat in Gujarat, western India, in 1608.

False Messiah
Any one of a number of pretenders who have over the centuries claimed to be the Messiah, or "anointed one," of Jewish tradition, sent by God to deliver humanity from the dominion of death and sin.

First Northern War
A war (1655–1660) in which Sweden invaded Poland with the help of Brandenburg-Prussia. Fear of Swedish expansion subsequently led Russia, Denmark, and the Holy Roman Empire to intervene, and few gains were made.

Forbidden City
The Imperial Palace built for the Ming emperors of China in their northern capital of Beijing. It was called the "Forbidden City" because access to the complex was barred to most people; the emperor alone could enter any part of the palace at will.

French and Indian Wars
A series of wars fought between 1689 and 1763 by British and French settlers in North America, together with their respective local allies. The separate phases are known as King William's War (1689–1697); Queen Anne's War (1702–1713); King George's War (1744–1748); and the American part of the Seven Years' War, usually known as the French and Indian War (1755–1763).

fresco
From the Italian word for "fresh," a method of painting with water-based colors directly onto freshly applied plaster. The artwork thus dries along with the plaster to become an integral part of the finished wall or ceiling.

Fronde
A series of civil wars in France from 1648 to 1653, waged by the nobility against the government of Cardinal Mazarin, chief minister during the minority of King Louis XIV.

Georgia
Country on the northeastern shore of the Black Sea. Under Safavid domination through much of the 16th century, it was taken by the Ottomans in the 1590s but restored by 1618.

Goa
Port city in western India bordering the Arabian Sea that became the capital of Portuguese India. After attacks by the Bijapur Sultanate and the Dutch the capital was moved to New Goa (Panaji) in 1759.

Gold Coast
A region of coastal West Africa roughly corresponding with modern Ghana. Named for its abundant gold reserves, it was rich in other minerals too, most notably copper and iron, and also became a center for the slave trade.

grand vizier
Title given to the Ottoman government officer in overall charge of the entire empire. Although he was generally a slave by birth or upbringing, his power often matched the sultan's.

Great Khanate
The largest and most easterly of the four Mongol khanates arising after the death of Genghis Khan. Initially covering much of modern China and Korea, it was ruled from Karakorum.

Great Zimbabwe
A stone-built fortified settlement on the Harare Plateau in the country that now bears its name. Built around 1200, it was the capital of a wealthy and powerful southern African empire with trading contacts as far afield as China.

Gujarat
Region of western India. An independent Muslim state from 1401, it was annexed by the Mughals in 1574 and overrun by the Marathas in the 18th century before falling under the control of the English East India Company from 1818 on.

guru
A Hindu, Buddhist, or Sikh spiritual leader. In Sikhism the term is specifically applied to the religion's ten founding patriarchs.

haiku
Japanese poetic form of 17 syllables (in three lines, with five, seven, and five syllables respectively). Popular in the Tokugawa period, its chief exponent was Matsuo Basho (1644–94).

Hapsburg Dynasty
Rulers of Austria from 1278 until 1918, who held the title of Holy Roman emperor in an unbroken line from 1438 until 1806. In the 16th and 17th centuries a branch of the Hapsburg family ruled the Spanish Empire.

Hausa
A people living in scattered communities along West Africa's Niger River who came together to form larger states from around 1200 A.D.

heretic
Someone who holds beliefs contrary to the accepted teaching of a church or religion.

Hinduism
The dominant religion and culture of India since ancient times. A complex system of beliefs and customs, it includes the worship of many gods and a belief in rebirth.

Holy League
A military alliance between Catholic Spain, Venice, and the Papacy that had the aim of expelling the Ottomans from Europe.

Holy Roman emperor
Title bestowed by the pope on a leading central European ruler, thought of as the chief secular champion of the Christian cause. The first Holy Roman emperor is usually held to have been the Frankish emperor Charlemagne, crowned in the year 800. The title was finally abolished by Napoleon Bonaparte in 1806.

Hormuz
A small but strategically vital island commanding the narrow strait where the Persian Gulf opens into the Indian Ocean. The newly established Safavid Empire was unable to prevent its occupation by the Portuguese in 1507, but finally recovered it in 1622.

Houses of Parliament
The legislature, or lawmaking assembly, of England since medieval times, comprising the House of Lords (nobility) and the House of Commons; also the building in London where they meet.

Hué
City on the Huong Estuary of southern Vietnam. It was the capital of the state of Annam under the Nguyen Dynasty, which controlled central and southern Vietnam from 1635 on.

Huguenots
French Protestants of the 16th and 17th centuries. The derivation of the name is uncertain.

Ife, Kingdom of
Kingdom established by the Yoruba people, based around the city of Ife in present-day Nigeria. Ife culture is characterized by splendid naturalistic sculptures made of bronze or wood.

Inquisition
Roman Catholic court set up in 1233 to suppress heresy (dissenting religious views). At first punishment was by excommunication; later fines, imprisonment, torture, and execution were used.

Iroquois Confederacy
League of five Iroquois-speaking peoples—the Mohawk, Oneida, Onondaga, Cayuga, and Seneca—who in the early 17th century inhabited much of modern New York state. Formed to end intertribal warfare, the confederacy proved a powerful force in conflicts with other Native American peoples. In the French and Indian Wars the Iroquois regularly sided with British forces against the French.

Islam
Literally meaning "surrender" to God's will, the faith based on the teachings of the Prophet Muhammad in 7th-century Arabia, and subsequently spread by military expansion and trade through much of West Asia and beyond. Its followers are known as Muslims.

Jamestown
The site in what is now Virginia of the first enduring British settlement in North America, established by an expedition sent out from England in 1607.

janissaries
The personal bodyguard of the Ottoman sultan (from the Turkish *yeniçeri*, meaning "new force"), recruited from Christian boys drafted to the sultan's court under the devshirme system.

Jesuit
A member of the Society of Jesus.

jihad
Derived from the Arabic term for "strive" or "fight," this word may refer simply to a moral or spiritual struggle but is also used to describe the waging of a holy war on the enemies of Islam.

jiziya
A tax levied by Islamic rulers on non-Muslim inhabitants of conquered lands.

Juchen
An alternative name for the Manchus, a Manchurian people who set up two separate dynasties in China, the first (the Jin) in 1126 and the second (the Qing) from 1644 on.

Kandy, Kingdom of
Independent monarchy in Sri Lanka that emerged at the end of the 15th century. After withstanding incursions by the Portuguese and Dutch, it was the last Sinhalese kingdom to fall to a colonial power when conquered by the British in 1818.

kaolin
A fine white clay mineral used in the manufacture of hard- and soft-paste porcelain and bone china.

Karelia
A region of northeastern Europe whose inhabitants are Finnish-speaking. Formerly an independent medieval state, it came under Swedish rule in the 17th century and was later ruled by Russia from 1721 to 1917, when it was divided between Finland and the Soviet Union.

Kashgar
Key trading center in Central Asia on the major caravan routes into the Ferghana Valley. Originally under Chinese control, it fell to the Mongols in 1219, was sacked by Timur the Lame in the late 14th century, and came under the rule of the Chinese Qing dynasty from 1755 on.

Khalka Mongols
Northern Mongol tribal grouping. After a rift with the Oirat Mongols they allied with the Manchus from the late 17th century until final defeat in 1759.

Khalsa Brotherhood
Community instituted in 1699 by the tenth Sikh guru Goband Singh as a race of warrior saints ready to die for the faith. The outward signs of membership are the so-called "five Ks": *kangha* (comb), *kacch* (cotton undershorts), *kirpan* (dagger), *kara* (steel bracelet), and *kesh* (uncut hair).

King James Bible
The English translation of the Bible published in 1611 on the orders of King James I; also known as the Authorized Version.

King William's War
The first conflict of the French and Indian Wars fought between British and French settlers in North America. Fighting broke out in connection with the European War of the League of Augsburg, in which France and Britain were enemies. The principal action of the war was the taking of Port Royal in Nova Scotia by the British in 1690.

Kokand, Khanate of
Islamic state in the western Ferghana Valley of Central Asia, founded in the early 16th century by the Uzbeks; it developed as a major trade center, with the city of Kokand as its capital from 1740. It was the last major khanate to fall to Russian expansion, in 1876.

Kongo, Kingdom of
Bantu-speaking kingdom south of the Congo River in central Africa. It survived until 1665, when it broke up following military defeat at the hands of the Portuguese.

Laos, Kingdom of
Buddhist kingdom in Southeast Asia that reached its zenith under King Souligna Vongsa (ruled 1637–1694) but split into three rival kingdoms (Vientiane, Luang Prabang, and Champasak) amid dynastic feuds from 1707 on.

liturgical
Relating to the liturgy, the form of public worship used in the Christian church.

Livonia
Region on the north coast of the Baltic Sea, equivalent to most of present-day Latvia and Estonia, that was ruled by the crusading order of the Teutonic Knights from the 13th to the 16th century, when it was divided between Poland and Sweden after the Livonian War with Russia (1558–1582).

Long Parliament
The English Parliament that was summoned by King Charles I in November 1640 and remained legally in being until it voted for its own dissolution in 1660.

lord protector
The title taken by Oliver Cromwell when he took charge of the government of England at the urging of the army in 1653, and which on his death in 1658 passed briefly to his son Richard Cromwell. This period of English history is known as the Protectorate.

Luba, Kingdom of
State in the upper Lomami Valley of eastern Angola that came to rule an empire of over 60,000 square miles (150,000 sq. km). The Luba claimed descent from divine ancestors, and their kings, deified at death, exercised a powerful hold over their subjects.

Lunda Empire
The Lunda Kingdom emerged in the 1670s in what is now eastern Angola to the west of Luba, which Lunda eventually eclipsed thanks to the wealth generated by the trade in copper and in slaves.

Macao
Port in southern China on the Pearl River estuary. Settled by the Portuguese in 1557, it became a key trade and missionary base; persecuted Japanese Christians sheltered there after the failed Shimabara rebellion (1637). Sovereignty over Macao reverted to China in 1999.

Manchus
Once-nomadic people from the Liaodong Peninsula in northeastern China. Formerly vassals of the Ming Dynasty, they grew in strength under Nurhachi (1559–1626) and won control of China (as the Qing Dynasty) in 1644.

Marathas

Hindu warrior people of western India who resisted external pressure under their dynamic leader Sivaji (1627–1680), warring with the Mughal Emperor Aurangzeb and the Bijapur Sultanate.

Matamba, Kingdom of

A state in the interior of what is now Angola whose rulers resisted European domination long after the coastal kingdoms had fallen in the 17th century, successfully playing off the Portuguese against the Dutch.

Mataram, Sultanate of

Kingdom in south–central Java that grew quickly under its first ruler, Sultan Agung (1613–1645), but came increasingly into conflict with the Dutch settlement at Batavia. It declined under subsequent rulers and was divided in 1755.

mausoleum

An elaborate building designed to house the tomb of a famous individual.

Mayflower Compact

An agreement drawn up on the *Mayflower*—the ship that brought the Pilgrims to New England in 1620—concerning the future government of the colony. It committed the settlers to self-government in accordance with the will of the majority.

Malacca

Also known as Melaka. Key port on the Strait of Malacca between the Indian and Pacific oceans that was the seat of an Islamic sultanate. Overrun by the Portuguese under Albuquerque in 1511, it became an important entrepot in the Moluccan spice trade and commerce with China. Malacca fell to the Dutch in 1641.

mercenary

A soldier who fights under the colors of a state other than his own for pay.

Merina

The earliest known inhabitants of Madagascar, who themselves may have immigrated from Indonesia. As a new wave of African settlers and foreign traders arrived on the island's coasts in the late 16th and early 17th centuries, a Merina Kingdom was established in the central highlands.

Ming Dynasty

The last indigenous Chinese dynasty (1368–1644), founded by Zhu Yuanzhang, who reconquered much territory from the Mongols (Yuan). It was supplanted by the Manchu (Qing) Dynasty.

mission

A religious foundation designed to spread a faith. Christian missions sponsored by the Spanish in the southern regions of North America and by the Jesuit order in the north played an important part in opening up North America to European penetration.

missionary

Someone who undertakes the task of spreading the Christian religion to unconverted peoples.

Mohicans

Algonquian-speaking Native American people inhabiting the Hudson River Valley who traded with early European settlers and engaged in a long and ultimately unsuccessful war with the neighboring Mohawks, members of the Iroquois Confederacy.

Molucca Islands

Group of islands in eastern Indonesia including Ceram, Ternate, and Amboina. As major producers of nutmeg, cloves, and mace, these "Spice Islands" were the focus of European trade and colonization from the early 16th century on. When the Dutch seized the Moluccas between 1595 and 1662, they gained a monopoly on the spice trade.

Mombasa, Sultanate of

Islamic sultanate, founded in 1592 on East Africa's Swahili Coast, whose ruler soon became a puppet of the Portuguese.

Moriscos

After the fall of Granada, the last Muslim stronghold in Spain (1492), the name given to Spanish Muslims who chose Christian baptism rather than exile and any of their descendants.

mosque

From the Arabic *masjid*, "place of prostration," the name given to a Muslim place of worship.

Mughal Dynasty

The ruling dynasty of the empire established by the Mughals, Islamic successors of Timur the Lame, who conquered northern India in 1526 and subsequently extended their rule over much of the subcontinent.

mulay

Literally "master," the title bestowed on Moroccan rulers of the Second Sharifian or Alawi sultanate.

Muscat

A seaport on the Gulf of Oman in the far southeast of the Arabian Peninsula that was hotly fought over by Portuguese and Ottoman forces through the 16th century.

Mwene Mutapa, Kingdom of

This northern Shona kingdom came to prominence after the collapse of Great Zimbabwe in the 15th Century. By 1500 it had conquered the states of Uteve and Mandanda, and made itself the main regional power.

Narragansett

Algonquian-speaking Native American people who inhabited much of Rhode Island in the early 17th century. The Narragansett aided the Massachusetts colonists in the Pequot War of 1637, but most were killed by colonists or resettled in the backlash following King Philip's War in 1676.

National Covenant

A covenant signed in 1638 by Scots opposed to the religious policies of King Charles I and in support of the Presbyterian church.

Navigation Acts

A series of protectionist laws passed by the British Parliament from 1651 to 1696 with the aim of boosting Britain's share of overseas trade by insisting that all imports had to be carried in British ships or in those of the country of origin.

New Amsterdam

The name given to New York City from 1626 to 1664, when it was occupied by Dutch settlers as the capital of the colony of New Netherland.

New England Confederation

Alliance of the colonies of Massachusetts Bay, Connecticut, New Haven, and Plymouth forged in 1643 for purposes of defense. Each colony kept its own independence in internal matters but agreed to consult on matters concerning "mutual safety and welfare." The confederation, which played an important part in coordinating the settlers' efforts in King Philip's War, was dissolved in 1684.

New France

Name given to the extensive territories in North America explored and settled by French colonists in the 16th to 18th centuries. At its peak in the early 18th century New France stretched from the Gulf of St. Lawrence to the Great Lakes and down the Mississippi Valley to the Gulf of Mexico.

New Model Army

An army created by Oliver Cromwell in 1644 to fight for Parliament against the king in the English Civil War. Well-trained and highly disciplined, it was a major force in defeating the Royalists, and it later had a political role under the Commonwealth and Protectorate.

New Netherland
Short-lived colony established along the Hudson River from 1621 on by the Dutch West India Company. The territory was taken over by the English in 1664, who divided it between the colonies of New York and New Jersey.

New Sweden
Short-lived Swedish colony on the Delaware River, comprising parts of modern Pennsylvania, New Jersey, and Delaware. Established by the New Sweden Company in 1638, it was overrun by Dutch settlers under Peter Stuyvesant in 1655.

New World
The Western Hemisphere, especially the continental landmasses of North and South America. The term was first used in the 16th century to distinguish the newly discovered lands of Europe's age of exploration from the "Old World" of Europe and Asia.

Northwest Passage
Sea passage from the Atlantic to the Pacific Ocean around the north coast of Canada, long sought unsuccessfully by explorers until finally traversed by the Norwegian Roald Amundsen from 1903 to 1906.

Oirat Mongols
People from the far west of Mongolia around Ulan Bator. Mongols who did not claim descent from Genghis Khan, they began to encroach on Xinjiang and Tibet in the 15th and 16th centuries, challenging the rule of China's Ming Dynasty. They were overwhelmed by the Manchus in 1759.

Olivares, Gaspar de Guzmán, Count Duke of
1587–1645. Chief minister of King Philip IV of Spain from 1621 to 1643 whose attempted reforms provoked a financial crisis and led to revolts in Catalonia and Portugal (then part of Spain).

Oman
A sheikhdom of southern Arabia whose rulers first threw the Portuguese out of Muscat, their stronghold on the Persian Gulf (1650), then took over their East African possessions, including Zanzibar and Mombasa (1698).

Orthodox church
Also known as the Eastern Orthodox church. The branch of the Christian church recognized throughout the Greek-speaking world of the eastern Mediterranean. Its spiritual head was, and is, the patriarch (archbishop) of Constantinople. The Slavs of eastern Europe and the Russians subsequently became part of the Orthodox church.

Ottoman Dynasty
Named for Uthman, a Turkic tribal leader who came to prominence in eastern Asia Minor in 1281, a line of rulers who built a great and enduring empire in western Asia and the eastern Mediterranean from the 14th century on.

Oyo, Kingdom of
A state in the interior of what is now western Nigeria whose warrior elite grew wealthy from the proceeds of the slave trade: They raided settlements in the surrounding countryside and traded slaves with visiting merchants on the coast.

Parliamentarian
A supporter of Parliament in the English Civil War; sometimes also called a Roundhead.

Parthenon
The temple of the goddess Athene on the Acropolis in Athens, which was built in the 5th century B.C.

pasha
The respectful title given to a vizier, senior military officer, or provincial governor under the Ottoman Empire. He often had considerable freedom of action on the ground.

Pegu, Kingdom of
Realm in southern Burma ruled from the city of Pegu, founded in 825 A.D. as the capital of the Mon kingdom and later ruled by the Toungou until the restoration of the Mons in the 1750s.

Pequots
Algonquian-speaking Native American people inhabiting the northeastern coast of Connecticut in the early 17th century. They came into conflict with English settlers and were defeated in the Pequot War of 1637.

Pilgrims
Name given to the English settlers who founded Plymouth Colony in Massachusetts in 1620.

Plymouth Company
A joint-stock company chartered in 1606 by King James I of England to found colonies in America between the latitudes of 38° and 45°N (in modern terms, from southern Maryland to the Canadian border). A colony established at the mouth of the Kennebec River in what is now Maine failed, and in 1620 the company was reorganized as the Plymouth Council for New England.

Podolia
A rich agricultural region of southwestern Ukraine, colonized by Polish settlers since the 14th century and annexed to Poland in 1430.

Pomerania
A region on either side of the mouth of the Oder River on the Baltic coast, now on the German–Polish border. An independent duchy in medieval times, it later became part of Brandenburg–Prussia, but was much disputed. In 1648 the western part of Pomerania was ceded to Sweden.

Port Royal
French settlement on the Bay of Fundy in what is now western Nova Scotia, founded by the sieur de Monts in 1605. The port was fiercely contested between French and English colonists, changing hands five times between 1605 and 1710, when it finally surrendered to a force from New England. The town is now known as Annapolis Royal.

Potala Palace
Huge former residence of the Dalai Lama in Lhasa, Tibet. The nine-story building stands on Potala Hill and was rebuilt in the 17th century.

Powhatan Confederacy
Alliance of Native American tribes under the leadership of Powhatan, established in coastal Virginia when the Jamestown colonists arrived in 1607. Relations with the newcomers were uneasy and broke into open violence in 1622, when Powhatan's successor organized a large-scale attack on the colony.

Presbyterian
A member of a church, such as the Presbyterian Church of Scotland, that is governed by elders of equal rank (presbyters) rather than by bishops and priests. The first Presbyterian church was established in Geneva, Switzerland, by the reformer John Calvin in 1541.

pretender
A person who claims that he or she has better legal right to a throne than the reigning monarch.

protectionism
The policy of protecting home industries by placing restrictions such as tariffs on foreign imports.

Protestant
Any of the churches, or their members, that broke with the Catholic church at the Reformation. Protestants originally took their name from the "Protestation" of the supporters of Martin Luther against the decision taken at the Diet of Speyer (1529) to reaffirm the edict of the Diet of Worms against Luther's teachings.

Protestant Union
An alliance of German Protestant rulers and cities formed in 1608 to defend their lands and rights against the Holy Roman emperor's attempts to reestablish Catholicism.

51

Puritan
A Christian of strict Protestant persuasion who opposed the role of bishops in the church hierarchy and sought a simple and plain form of worship.

Qing Dynasty
Final Chinese imperial dynasty (1644–1912); its zenith was under Kangxi and Qianlong (1654–1792), when China reached its greatest territorial extent, stretching from Turkistan in the west to the island of Taiwan in the east.

Qosot Mongols
One of the four constituent tribes of the Oirat Mongols; their leader, Gushri Khan, helped the fifth Dalai Lama attain power in Tibet by overthrowing the king of Tsang in 1642.

Quakers
Members of the Society of Friends.

Rajputs
Hindu landowning class of northwest India (Rajputana, later Rajasthan). Rising to prominence from the 9th century and reaching their height in the early 16th, they ruled such cities as Jodhpur and Jaipur. Akbar allowed them independence within the Mughal Empire, and they subsequently ruled as autonomous princes under the British Raj.

rationalism
Reliance on reason and experience rather than faith or superstition as the means of explaining the world and discovering knowledge.

republican
Someone who believes that power should be held by the people or their elected representatives, not by a monarch ruling with an aristocracy.

Restoration
The reestablishment of the monarchy in England with the assumption of power by King Charles II, son of the deposed Charles I, in 1660.

Rhenish Palatinate
A state on the Rhine River in Germany ruled by a hereditary ruler called the prince palatine. The princes of the Palatinate were the leaders of the Protestant movement in Germany before and during the Thirty Years' War.

Romanov Dynasty
The dynasty that ruled Russia from the accession of Michael Romanov in 1613 until the overthrow of the last czar, Nicholas II, in 1917.

Royalist
A supporter of King Charles I in the English Civil War.

Royal Society
The oldest, and still the leading, scientific society in Britain, which received its charter from King Charles II in 1662.

Rozwi Dynasty
A dynasty of Shona chiefs that established itself in the southwest of the Zimbabwe plateau in the mid 17th century. They grew wealthy by exacting tribute from those trading across their territories.

Russo-Polish War
A war (1654–1667) that arose after Cossacks living in Polish-ruled Ukraine rebelled and placed themselves under Russian protection.

Saadi Dynasty
A line of Arab rulers who originated in Arabia but eventually came to prominence in Morocco. Taking Marrakesh in 1525 and Fez in 1550, they made Morocco prosperous, maintaining diplomatic and trading relations with both the Islamic and Christian worlds.

Safavid Dynasty
Beginning with Esmail I in 1501, this Persian dynasty came to rule over not only Iran but also Armenia, Georgia, and parts of Uzbekistan, Turkmenistan, Azerbaijan, and Afghanistan. Esmail's support for the minority Shiite branch of Islam had a profound impact on the region's subsequent history.

Senegambia
The area of West Africa between the Senegal and Gambia rivers.

serf
A laborer who was not free to move from the land on which he worked.

shah
Persian for "king." Originally the title of the kings of Persia, it also came to be used by the rulers of other countries in South and Central Asia

Shiism
The faith of the Shia-i Ali, the "Party of Ali," Muslims claiming allegiance to Muhammad's son-in-law and to those imams believed to be his spiritual successors.

Shimabara Rebellion
Uprising that broke out in 1637 on the Shimabara Peninsula, near Nagasaki, Japan, when indigenous Christians led by Amakusa Shiro sought to protest the harsh rule of Tokugawa Ieyasu.

shogun
Literally "commander of the imperial guard," the title given from 1192 on to the leader of Japan's ruling warrior family. For almost seven centuries the shoguns were the true rulers of Japan, leaving the country's emperors to occupy themselves primarily with ceremonial duties.

Sibir, Khanate of
Tatar khanate in western Siberia that arose in the early 16th century from the disintegration of the Khanate of the Golden Horde. Russian encroachment began with the capture by Cossacks of its capital, Kashlyk, in 1582.

Sikhism
A religion founded in the Punjab area of northwestern India by Nanak (1469-1539). Sikhs believe in one god who is the creator of the universe and in the equality of all human beings.

Society of Friends
A Christian sect founded in England in the mid-17th century. Its beliefs include nonviolence, the rejection of set forms of worship, and simplicity of dress and speech. Its members are known as Quakers.

Songhai Empire
A trading empire centered on the city of Gao in what is now northwestern Nigeria. Long overshadowed by the power of Mali to the west, it emerged to eclipse Mali in the 15th century.

States-General
The legislative assembly of the Dutch Republic.

Stuart Dynasty
The royal house of Scotland from 1371 and of England from the accession of James VI of Scotland to the English throne in 1603 until 1714.

Sufi
A Muslim mystic who attempts, through intense meditation or a trance state brought on by repetitive prayer, music, or (in the case of the "whirling dervishes") dance, to transcend worldly concerns and find spiritual enlightenment.

sultan
Taken from the Arabic word for "power" or "authority," this title is often loosely applied to any Muslim ruler but is associated especially with the emperors of the Ottoman Dynasty.

Sunni
A member of the largest sect of Islam, which believes that the first three caliphs were rightful successors to Muhammad, and that religious guidance should come from the Koran and other scriptures, not from a human authority.

Swahili Coast
Area of the East African seaboard along which for many centuries African peoples traded and intermarried with Arab traders, and where a distinctive, hybrid culture grew up, epitomized by the half-African, half-Arabic Swahili language.

Swiss Confederation
League of Swiss cantons (states) that came together to defeat their Hapsburg overlords in the 14th and 15th centuries.

Taj Mahal
Marble mausoleum in Agra, northern India, built by the Mughal Emperor Shah Jahan as a monument to his dead wife Mumtaz Mahal. Some 20,000 workers took 22 years (from 1632 to 1653) to complete it.

Tatars
Also known as Tartars. Name given to various originally nomadic peoples of the Central Asian steppes. Most often applied to the subjects of the Khanate of the Golden Horde and their descendants in Russia, it sometimes also encompasses other Mongol and Turkic groups.

Ten Gurus
Patriarchs of the Sikh religion, which arose in the Punjab region of northwestern India in the late 15th century.

theocracy
Government by a priesthood. In theocratic states adherence to the tenets of a faith determines the political and legal system. Tibet under the Dalai Lama was a theocracy from the 1640s until its annexation by China in the 1950s.

Time of Troubles
A period of intense unrest in Russia (1598–1613) marked by peasant and Cossack revolts, foreign invasion, and civil war. It ended with the election of Michael Romanov as czar.

Tokugawa Shogunate
Japan's third and final dynasty of shoguns (warrior rulers), founded in 1603 by Tokugawa Ieyasu, who wrested control from the daimyos (territorial governors). Under 15 successive rulers it brought peace and stability at the cost of isolating Japan from the rest of the world. The shogunate ended with the restoration of imperial rule in 1867 (the Meiji Restoration).

Torwa Kingdom
A Shona state with its capital at Khama, 150 miles (240 km) to the west of Great Zimbabwe. Torwa's wealth was based on the large-scale mining of gold. It reached its height in the mid-17th century.

Toungou Dynasty
Dynasty that unified Burma from 1539 on after the collapse of the state of Pagan. Its greatest rulers, Tabinshweti and Bayinnaung, subdued the Shans and Mons. The realm lost ground to neighboring powers in the 17th century, when Burma fragmented into a multitude of smaller states.

Tran Ninh
Upland region in north–central Laos, also known as Xiangkhoang.

Triple Alliance
An alliance forged in 1668 between the Dutch Republic, England, and, Sweden to wage the War of Devolution against France.

Tungus
Also known as the Evenks. Indigenous people of the taiga (subarctic forest) of eastern Siberia, who lived by hunting, fishing, and reindeer herding.

Turkmen
Tent-dwelling pastoral nomads living east of the Caspian Sea along the borders of Afghanistan and Iran.

United Provinces
The seven allied provinces—Friesland, Gelderland, Groningen, Holland, Overijseel, Utrecht, and Zeeland—that made up the Dutch Republic.

Uzbeks
Nomadic pastoralists (herders) of Turkic origin inhabiting the steppes of Central Asia, in particular the area now known as Uzbekistan.

Van Diemen's Land
Former name of the island of Tasmania off Australia's southern coast. Originally named by the Dutch explorer Abel Tasman for his patron Anthony van Diemen, the governor of Batavia, it was given its present name in 1855.

Versailles
A vast palace built for King Louis XIV southwest of Paris, one of the glories of French classical architecture. From 1682 Louis spent most of his time at Versailles and expected his nobles to spend much of the year there too.

Virgin of Guadalupe
Seen in a vision by a native Mexican in 1531, Our Lady of Guadalupe became the focus of a Catholic cult that made her shrine in central Mexico the most important pilgrimage site in Latin America.

Wampanoag
Algonquian speaking Native American people inhabiting the coastal areas of Massachusetts at the time of arrival of the first English colonists. The Wampanoag never recovered from defeat by the settlers in King Philip's War (1675–1676).

War of the League of Augsburg
The war (1689–1697) between Louis XIV of France and the League of Augsburg, an alliance first formed in 1686 and consisting of Emperor Leopold I, Spain, Sweden, and Bavaria, later joined by Britain, the Dutch Republic, and Savoy.

West India Company (Dutch)
Company chartered by the States-General (parliament) of the Dutch Republic in 1621 to exploit trade with the Americas. It had extensive operations in Brazil (finally lost to the Portuguese in 1654) and in coastal North America, where its lands were taken over by the British in 1664. Its achievements included the founding of New Amsterdam—today's New York City.

William of Orange
Stadtholder (chief magistrate) of the Netherlands who married Mary, the daughter of King James II of England. When James's pro-Catholic policies alienated his Protestant subjects, a group of prominent politicians invited William to land in England in 1688 and depose the king. William was crowned joint monarch with Mary as King William III of Britain in February 1689.

Zanzibar, Sultanate of
The Muslim state established by the rulers of Oman after they captured the island of Zanzibar, just off the African coast, from the Portuguese in 1698. Their victory put an end to Portugal's 200-year presence in East Africa and restored the old order on the Swahili Coast.

Zunghar Mongols
Leading tribe of the Oirat Mongols that tried but failed to unite the Mongols against the Manchus. Oirat forces under their leader Galdan were crushed by the Manchus in 1696.

FURTHER READING

Bobrick, Benson. *East of the Sun: The Epic Conquest and Tragic History of Siberia*. New York, NY: Henry Holt and Co, 1993.

Boxer, Charles. *The Dutch Seaborne Empire 1600–1800*. New York, NY: Penguin, reprint edn., 1992.

Caffrey, Kate. *The Mayflower*. New York, NY: Stein & Day, 1974.

Coward, Barry. *Oliver Cromwell*. New York, NY: Longman, 199s.

Dunlop, Ian. *Louis XIV*. New York, NY: St. Martin's Press, 2000.

Forsyth, James. *A History of the Peoples of Siberia: Russia's North Asian Colony 1581–1990*. New York, NY: Cambridge University Press, 1992.

Hall, Alfred Rupert. *The Revolution in Science 1500–1750*. New York, NY: Longman, 3rd edn., 1983.

Hellyer, Marcus. ed. *The Scientific Revolution: The Essential Readings*. Malden, MA: Blackwell Publishers, 2003.

Hill, Christopher. *The World Turned Upside Down: Radical Ideas during the English Revolution*. New York, NY: Penguin, reprint edn., 1984.

Hsu, Immanuel Chung-Yueh. *The Rise of Modern China*. New York, NY: Oxford University Press, 6th edn., 2000.

Hutton, Ronald. *The Restoration: A Political and Religious History of England and Wales 1658–1667*. New York, NY: Oxford University Press, 1985.

Israel, Jonathan. *The Dutch Republic: Its Rise, Greatness, and Fall 1477–1806*. New York, NY: University Press, reprint edn., 1998.

Jansen, Marius. *The Making of Modern Japan*. Cambridge, MA: Belknap Press, 2002.

Jansen, Marius. *Warrior Rule in Japan*. New York, NY: Cambridge University Press, 1995.

Kessler, Lawrence. *K'ang-hsi and the Consolidation of Ch'ing Rule*. Chicago, IL: University of Chicago Press, 1976.

Ladurie, Emmanuel Le Roy. *Saint-Simon and the Court of Louis XIV*. Chicago, IL: University of Chicago Press, 2001.

Longworth, Philip. *The Cossacks*. New York, NY: Holt, Rinehart & Winston, 1970.

Middleton, Richard. *Colonial America: A History 1565–1776*. Malden, MA: Blackwell Publishers, 3rd revised edn., 2002.

Mitford, Nancy. *The Sun King*. New York, NY: Penguin, reprint edn., 1994.

Morgan, David. *Medieval Persia 1040–1797*. New York, NY: Longman, 1988.

Nash, Gary B. *Red, White, and Black: The Peoples of Early America*. Upper Saddle River, NJ: Prentice Hall, 4th edn., 1999.

Parker, Geoffrey, ed. *The Thirty Years' War*. New York, NY: Routledge, 2nd edn., 1997.

Parker, Geoffrey. *The Dutch Revolt*. London, UK: Allen Lane, 1977.

Peterson, Willard J. *The Cambridge History of China Vol.9 Part 1: The Ch'ing Dynasty to 1800*. New York, NY: Cambridge University Press, 2001.

Reid, Anna. *The Shaman's Coat: A Native History of Siberia*. New York, NY: Walker & Co., 2002.

Russell, Conrad. *The Causes of the English Civil War*. New York, NY: Oxford University Press, 1990.

Sansom, G.B. *A History of Japan 1615–1867*. Stanford, CA: Stanford University Press, 1958.

Savory, Roger. *Iran under the Safavids*. New York, NY: Cambridge University Press, 1980.

Schama, Simon. *The Embarrassment of Riches: An Interpretation of Dutch Culture in the Golden Age*. New York, NY: Vintage, 1997.

Shimizu, Yoshiaki, ed. *Japan: The Shaping of Daimyo Culture 1185–1868*. Wasington, DC: The National Gallery of Art, 1988.

Spence, Jonathan D. *Emperor of China: Self-Portrait of K'ang-Hsi*. New York, NY: Vintage Books, reissue edn., 1988.

Taylor, Alan. *American Colonies: The Settling of North America*. New York, NY: Penguin, new edn., 2002.

Wedgwood, C.V. *The Thirty Years' War*. New York, NY: New York Review Books, reprint edn., 2005.

Welch, Anthony. *Shah Abbas and the Arts of Isfahan*. New York, NY: The Asia Society, 1973.

Wedgwood, C.V. *The King's War 1641–1647*. New York, NY: Macmillan, 1959.

Zumthor, Paul. *Daily Life in Rembrandt's Holland*. Stanford, CA: Stanford University Press, 1994.

SET INDEX

61